MAN AND SECURITY

MAN AND SECURITY

HARRY L. HECKEL

Troitsa Books
Commack, New York

Editorial Production: Susan Boriotti
Office Manager: Annette Hellinger
Graphics: Frank Grucci and Jennifer Lucas
Information Editor: Tatiana Shohov
Book Production: Donna Dennis, Patrick Davin, Christine Mathosian
and Tammy Sauter
Circulation: Maryanne Schmidt
Marketing/Sales: Cathy DeGregory

Library of Congress Cataloging-in-Publication Data

Heckel, Harry L.
Man and inner security / by Harry L. Heckel III.
p.   cm.
ISBN 1-56072-483-8
1. Religion--Philosophy. 2. Philosophy and social sciences. 3. Peace of
mind. 4. Spiritual life. I. Title.
B151.H385   1997   97-40507
210--dc21   CIP

Copyright © 1999 by Harry L. Heckel
Troitsa Books, a division of
Nova Science Publishers, Inc.
6080 Jericho Turnpike, Suite 207
Commack, New York 11725
Tele. 516-499-3103   Fax 516-499-3146
e-mail: Novascience@earthlink.net
e-mail: Novasci1@aol.com
Web Site: http://www.nexusworld.com/nova

All rights reserved. No part of this book may be reproduced, stored in a retrieval system
or transmitted in any form or by any means: electronic, electrostatic, magnetic, tape,
mechanical photocopying, recording or otherwise without permission from the
publishers.

The authors and publisher have taken care in preparation of this book, but make no
expressed or implied warranty of any kind and assume no responsibility for any errors
or omissions. No liability is assumed for incidental or consequential damages in
connection with or arising out of information contained in this book.

This publication is designed to provide accurate and authoritative information with
regard to the subject matter covered herein. It is sold with the clear understanding that
the publisher is not engaged in rendering legal or any other professional services. If
legal or any other expert assistance is required, the services of a competent person
should be sought. FROM A DECLARATION OF PARTICIPANTS JOINTLY ADOPTED BY
A COMMITTEE OF THE AMERICAN BAR ASSOCIATION AND A COMMITTEE OF
PUBLISHERS.

Printed in the United States of America

To

Kathleen and Sara

And

To

Mom (the Religion Major) and Dad (the Chemist)
Whose Dinner Conversations Gave Me the Questions

Not every one that saith unto me, Lord, Lord, shall enter into the kingdom of Heaven; but he that doeth the will of my Father which is in Heaven.

Many will say to me in that day, Lord, Lord, have we not prophesied in thy name? and in thy name have cast out devils? and in thy name have done many wonderful works?

And the will I profess unto them, I never knew you: depart from me, ye that work iniquity.

(Matthew 7:21-23)

Contents

PREFACE

Does it make sense that the Creator of the Universe would have designed and ordered everything except human behavior? We see the Big Bang Theory as proof of a Creator because it describes the complex interactions of the laws of the physical sciences.

Natural Laws of Human Behavior would be rules that maximize the probability of our survival as a species. From the beginning of our lives we are taught how to behave. Before we know to search objectively for the laws of human behavior, it is too late. Nevertheless, just because pre-conceived notions cloud our discovery ability does not mean those laws do not exist. Even if we can not define these laws, we should be able to recognize them.

I guess most of us think of philosophy as a group of logically linked ideas that seem to make sense, and religion as a group of logically linked thoughts that make us feel good. The heart of this book is the scientific method. I am trying to scientifically prove a theory. Not by stating that archaeological digs prove the Bible is history, but by looking at the rules Jesus gave us for life on earth and proving these are the Natural Laws of Human Behavior. Although the techniques of science involve test tubes and experiments, the accuracy of a theory is determined by its ability to describe the real environment. The proof of the accuracy of the laws of Jesus is whether they describe the method for man to survive as a species and maximize the individual's quality of life over time.

When I was a child, our Sunday dinners often featured a discussion between Dad, who has a Ph.D. in chemistry and doesn't believe in superstition, and Mom, who majored in religion. For me, just starting school in the fifties, the "accept on faith" religion of my mother was disturbed by the educational accent of science's "prove it" after the Soviet launch of the first satellite. Then in the sixties we had all this idealism of what things should be and the realization that they weren't and we wanted to know where we were going and how to get there. Wasn't there a scientific answer to all this?

This is a philosophy of self-interest mashed together with the self-sacrifice and denial of Christianity within a middle-class Protestant. Although this book says that each of us should do what is best for ourselves, it just so happens that its description of what is best for ourselves is a lot like what you were taught in Sunday School class, with a few differences.

I suppose it was inevitable that some baby boomer growing up in the sixties would write a book like this. We had so many questions without scientific answers. It would be nice to think that as we grow older and look for the spiritualism humanity seeks in old age; it would be nice to think we can find that spiritualism with a scientific justification.

My thanks to my sons, especially the oldest, for their critical reading of this document. My thanks also to my sister Florence for her editing prior to finding a publisher, and to my daughter-in-law Heather and my friend Ann Burns for their critical reading of this document.

Chapter One

A PHILOSOPHY OF SCIENCE AND THEORY

Is there a way to act and a way to think that is BETTER than any other way? And what do we mean by BETTER? Most importantly, can this be proven, instead of being someone's logical or degreed opinion?

There seems to be no logical base for the rules of our religion and no morality to our scientific logic. Would the Creator of the universe have included laws of human behavior in His design? Why not? There are laws of chemistry and physics. For instance, we know water always boils at the same temperature under the same conditions. Aren't there also laws of human behavior?

There are various philosophies of life based on a little observation and much logic. They all seem to contradict each other and none can really prove itself to be true. Anyone can link a chain of logic together that will tell you how to act. They can base this chain on anything—their impression of human behavior, their desire for revenge on a stereotype, or their dreams. We are left hanging in mid-nothing with only idle speculation. What is needed is a method to discover laws of human behavior.

There appears to be one accurate methodology. It is the scientific method which scientists have used to discover natural laws of physics, chemistry, and the other physical and natural sciences. This philosophy of science has given us the technology of the world we live in.

Science is trying to discover reality—the environment as it really is, not just as you perceive it at the moment, but as we all perceive it or can perceive it. There are two environments—the one that actually exists and the one your senses tell you is there. You can not perceive everything, only what is immediately around you that you can hear, feel, taste, smell, or see. Science is trying to discover the real environment; what is actually there. It is trying to define the things we can observe, such as an apple falling from a tree, and the things we can not directly observe, such as two atoms of hydrogen and an atom of oxygen combined in a molecule of water.

The scientific method is in the first chapter of every science book you had in high school. The method seems quite simple. The scientist first observes something. This may be anything—an object in a test tube, or an apple falling from a tree. Whatever he has observed, the scientist thinks about it and states an hypothesis which tries to explain what happened. Further observations are made to determine the accuracy of the hypothesis and, if necessary, it will be changed. With further observations, its accuracy and predictability may be so great as to have it recognized as a law of nature.

According to Norman Campbell (What is Science?, 1953, Dover Publication, Inc, New York; first published by Methuen & Co., Ltd. in 1921), a natural law is an "invariable association" between "events or properties" (p.49) about which there is "universal agreement" (p.27).

That "invariable association" means an occurrence has been observed several times and was not just one unusual phenomenon. Furthermore, it must happen every time the "events or properties" occur. Every time two parts hydrogen are combined with one part oxygen (under the same standard conditions) the result must be water.

How do we know our hypothesis was not just our perception of the environment? How do we know it is the real environment? To be considered accurate, the law must acquire what Campbell calls, "universal agreement". Accuracy is not in the mind of the observer, but must be verified in the mind of all observers (more or less). Universal agreement ensures that the real environment is being observed, not just one person's perception of the environment.

The proof of a natural law is that it must describe the real environment. The law is proved if it describes something that happens every time under the same conditions and everyone agrees that it happens every time under those conditions.

More than discovering natural laws, science explains them using theories. According to Campbell, "A theory ... is some proposition which satisfies these conditions: (1) It must be such that the laws which it is devised to explain can be deduced from it; (2) it must explain those laws in the sense of introducing ideas which are more familiar or, in some other way, more acceptable than those of the laws; (3) it must predict new laws and these laws must turn out to be true." (p.89) Laws and theories are not the same. Theories are a teaching device to explain the laws so we have a better understanding of them and can, therefore, make better use of them. Theories are also used to discover new laws.

"The explanation offered by a theory ... is always based on an analogy, and the system with which an analogy is traced is always one of which the laws are known". (Campbell, p.96) Again, "the explanation offered by a theory is always based on an analogy with laws". (Campbell, p.97) For instance, "the immense theory involved in the whole science of geology explains the structure of the earth as it exists to-day by supposing that this structure is the result of the age-long operation of influences, the action of which is described by laws observable in modern conditions." (Campbell, p.96) Again, "The theory of evolution explains the laws involved in the assertion that there are such-and-such living beings by supposing that these living beings are the descendants of others whose characters have been modified by reaction to their surroundings in a manner which is described by laws applicable to living beings at the present day." (Campbell, p.96)

The laws to be deduced from these theories are themselves based on logic as a tool to explain an "invariable association" between "events or properties". Darwin looked at all those strange creatures and drew a logical conclusion. A theory explains these laws. So, of course, the laws can be deduced from the theory. The critical parts of a theory are the analogy and the prediction of new laws. Darwin never witnessed evolution, only its results. His theory is based on other natural laws created by observations of animal behavior.

There is no definitive reason, no absolute truth, that states that analogy is an accurate means of creating theories. If everything in the universe is part of a large design, so that everything is, in some way, related; then analogy is a good way of finding theories. Analogy, however, can not be considered the proof of a theory; it is just a logic tool to propose new theories.

Some descriptions of the scientific method include in the proof of a theory, its ability to predict future occurrences. Prediction, for instance, means stating that if two parts hydrogen are combined with one part oxygen under these specific conditions the result will be water.

Prediction, according to Campbell, is not philosophically possible. Nevertheless, one important part of deciding which theory is correct is to find the one that is able "to predict true laws and the others are not. It is for this reason that prediction by theories is so fundamentally important." (p.107) For Campbell, prediction means finding new laws by using the theory and then proving these laws by gaining universal agreement on their correct description of the real environment. This is an important part of proving the theory.

This idea that theories based on existing laws can be used to find new laws implies that all things are related. The Big Bang theory recognizes that everything in the universe came from one event and implies that all natural laws must fit together. If two laws conflicted with one another, the universe would have a broken spring; it would not work. The Creator of the Universe must have put it all together correctly. This means that all laws work with all other laws. They do not conflict; they complement each other.

There are times when two different theories appear to be accurate. For instance, there is the story of the witch doctor and the weatherman. Every spring the village gave a goat to the witch doctor. The villagers had always known this would insure a good harvest. If the harvest was bad, the goat had been one with evil spirits in it. The weatherman could also explain why the harvest was good or bad. Furthermore his theories considered more than the clouds. They also considered the wind, average temperature, etc. These things affect each other. The theory that accurately applies to more related phenomena is proven and disproves other theories covering a smaller group of related phenomena. This is the concept of scope. Scope is the idea that the theory that relates the most phenomena, and still describes reality, is the correct theory.

The scientific method seems to have one glaring inadequacy. It predicts the future based on past performance. It assumes that the laws of nature will never change. However, it does not attempt to prove that they will never change. It states, for instance, that an apple will always fall down off a tree and it will even state how fast the apple will fall. With a little imagination, a person could see that it is not necessarily so, that because something has happened; it will continue to happen. Of course, the scientific method has always worked.

The solution to possible changing laws of nature is to prove the existence of a control. If the universe is governed by rules of chaos, the future is not predictable. Chaos means there are no natural laws. If there are no natural laws, the scientific method is not a valid means of creating theories. Of course, neither is any other method valid. Without theories we can draw no conclusions about how man acts or how he should act. No-theory may have accuracy since a person could call everything either luck or fate. Scope, however, is totally lacking since the nature of no-theory is that no one occurrence is related to any other occurrence. Disproving chaos can be done by any accurate theory with a minimum of scope. So, any idea of a control is easy to prove.

It is well to remember that there are many things to be studied. When examining the scope of a theory, consider the strength of the relationship between the phenomena being explained. Scope is not just covering numbers of phenomena, it is covering a group of strongly related phenomena. The weatherman was accurate because he could also explain thunderstorms, hurricanes, etc.

Do not be lured into accepting an idea because it has great scope. An accurate description of the real environment is the first consideration; scope is the second.

In the early days, the philosophers of science searched for definitive, absolute laws. They were sure that each new law was the last word on that subject. Then, as more research was done and more discoveries were made, the idea of finding unchangeable laws had to be discarded. Too often those new discoveries created qualifiers for existing laws. After all, water does not always boil at 212 degrees Fahrenheit. It only does that at sea level; actually, at a specific air pressure; actually, only if it is pure water. One of the reasons for this is scope. Those things that are related to each other keep affecting each other in a dizzyingly complex manner. Since everything is related in some fashion, it is all very challenging.

It is one thing to discover laws about boiling water: it is quite another to discover laws of human nature. The problem is the "human factor". We have been taught human behavior all our life. Each of us knows what is correct and proper. The problem is that each culture has different definitions of what correct and proper are. The observer can not make an unbiased opinion because he has been taught to be biased.

Fortunately, it is not necessary for the proof of a law that the law be discovered using academically correct techniques. Indeed, many scientific discoveries have been accidental. Proof only requires that the law describe the real environment. It does not matter where the law came from.

As for laws of human behavior, why would the Creator design these laws if the humans could not recognize and use them? If the Creator wants us to have the laws, He will have to give them to us. Has He already done this?

Since the purpose of the laws is to describe the real environment, the proof is only concerned with this, nothing else. In trying to teach rational explanations, it becomes necessary, at times, to add ideas that form logical bridges between the beginning idea and where the philosopher wants to go. It appears to me that this is a fairly dangerous exercise, because the theory ends up describing the philosopher's logic and not reality. Only those things that affect or will affect people are relevant to people. This is the boundary within which all meaningful laws and theories must exist. There needs to be at least one absolute truth to make a judgement. Relevance is that truth. Therefore, accurate laws and theories must be relevant: They must describe what affects people and will affect people.

Since a theory on human behavior must be relevant, it must include the future. This is important. A theory on human behavior must not just describe what is good for us at present. It must describe what is going to continue to be good for us in the future. Jumping off a cliff is a hypothesis that will give us a great feeling now—weightlessness and a terrific view, but in the long run, such a hypothesis is not to our benefit; it has its down side.

We think of natural laws as working instantaneously. When hydrogen and oxygen are added together and a spark is fired, there is an explosion and the result is water. It is all very quick. Not all laws work that quickly. The deterioration of radioactive materials into lead can take thousands of years. The extinction of species by the law of the survival of the fittest can take hundreds of years. The effects of the natural laws of human behavior may take many years to become apparent.

If there are natural laws of human behavior, aren't we just the puppets of those laws just like hydrogen and oxygen in the presence of a spark? Doesn't this mean we have no free will? Of course, we think we have free will. And, we do. The environment, situation, we find ourselves in now is the result of natural laws, but what we do starting now, is our decision. Occurrences of the past and present can cause you harm, but actions you take now can give you benefits now and in the future. There is nothing in the laws that says we have no choice. The laws simply state that there are results to those choices.

The results of one action can be combated by another, so that the actions and thoughts that caused you harm can be replaced by those that benefit you. Our whole lives are spent making thoughts and actions. Some are good and some are bad. Our present environment is the result of the natural laws of human behavior that are caused by our thoughts and actions plus the results of other people's thoughts and actions and all the other laws of the universe. If your home is destroyed by an earthquake, that had nothing to do with whether you are a bad person.

Proving the accuracy of laws of human behavior is difficult, because human affairs shift rapidly from day-to-day, and any continuing trend may take decades to become noticeable. For the individual, who can observe most closely his own existence, seeing the accuracy of laws of human behavior will be easier. The accuracy of these laws will be decided by the person most affected by them—you!

It would be nice to have some help to show what the laws are and whether they are accurate. This is the job of the theory—to offer an explanation, not to prove the laws, but to allow us to understand what we are looking at, to decide on its accuracy.

Why is the Creator putting us through all this? It seems to be very difficult to discover the reasons why things work in this universe. And, when we do discover something, we can not be sure that we will not discover something else which will qualify what we have just found. Couldn't the Creator of the universe have made things a little easier? It's as if nothing will ever be so certain that the decision will be forced upon us. Each of us will have to make decisions for ourselves.

Knowing the laws that are relevant to us is important, not the reasons for them. After all, when you let go of something, it falls down. Your knowledge of gravity does not affect whether it will fall. Perhaps there are things about our universe that are too complicated for us. That is not important.

To summarize, if our universe is designed, if there are Natural Laws of Human Behavior, perhaps we can find an answer to our moral questions. We are looking for a description of the real environment, now and in the future, not just the environment we can perceive at this moment in time. We can not discover these laws, because we can not observe without distorting the results with our own preconceived perceptions. Fortunately, how laws are discovered is not related to their accuracy. A theory to explain these laws, to help us judge their accuracy, must be logically sound enough so that the laws could be logically deduced from the theory. The theory must explain by using an analogy with known laws and theories. The theory must define and predict other, accurate laws. Finally, maybe, there will be universal agreement on Natural Laws of Human Behavior.

Chapter Two

FIRST THEORY OF SECURITY

What are we? Why do we act the way we do? One thing is obvious: we are living organisms. We may be special living organisms, but we are still living organisms. This means that we are made of chemicals and function by chemical reactions. We act and think by means of chemical messages being sent between our brain and the other parts of our body.

These chemical reactions are controlled by our genes. Genes control the way we look and the way we feel when we are hungry. They control our need for sex so that we have children and the species continues. Genes control the way we react to our environment.

We react chemically to what we sense through hearing, sight, smell, taste, and feel. We react to food, sun (possibly by getting a sunburn), and bad air. We react chemically to internal stimulation when our temperature rises to fight disease and when our stomach reminds us it's time to eat. Our sense of touch measures pain; our sense of smell is irritated by noxious fumes; loud noise hurts our ears; bright lights hurt our eyes; and our sense of taste warns us of food that is not good for us. We react to the sound of someone yelling, the sight of a car swerving sharply toward us, the taste of lemons, and the feel of a slimy clam.

Our senses are stimulated from two sources. One is our genetic makeup which causes us to breathe, digest our food, grow, and reproduce. The other source of stimulation is our environment. This is the bright light that causes us to squint, the smell of delicious food that causes us to go into the kitchen, the good-looking person that causes us to glance, and the on-rushing truck that causes us to leap aside. We act the way we do because our environment and our genes stimulate us, causing us to react chemically. Our environment and our genetic makeup govern our behavior.

An organism's chemical reactions must cause the organism to function in such a way that it survives and reproduces. Otherwise, its species will become extinct. The behavior that allows an organism to act so that it survives is partially genetically controlled instinct and partially an ability to react properly to the environment.

Ants are an example of an organism controlled by instinct. Each ant is born with a set pattern of behavior. It follows that pattern and does not deviate from it. A worker ant forages for food. A queen ant lays eggs. The worker does not lay eggs and the queen does not forage for food.

Not all living organisms have their behavior so strongly controlled by genetic makeup. If human beings behaved totally by instinct, we would all act the same way. When we say that no two people are alike, we say that man has little or no instinct. An instinct-controlled animal does almost no learning since it knows everything it needs to know. Man is born knowing almost nothing and has to spend many years learning before he can take care of himself.

The higher forms of animal life live in too varied and competitive an environment to survive on instinct. They have to learn and use that knowledge to adapt to the changing conditions in which they find themselves. It takes a lion two years to reach maturity. Baby lions do not know how to hunt instinctively; they must be taught. An instinct-controlled lion could not survive.

There is some controversy as to whether human beings evolved or were created. The question is irrelevant. It is not necessary to say that human beings evolved. It is only necessary to note that we have been around for a long time, and we have survived well. Surviving in nature has meant that we are subject to the same laws of nature as any other living organism which means there is something in the genetic makeup of the individual human being which allows our species to survive.

Survival means evaluating the environment and reacting to it. The perceived environment is anything that we can detect as affecting us. It is made up of the things we see in the room we are in. If someone is yelling at us, that is part of our environment. If we are dreaming, the dream is part of our environment. When we sleep, the dreams are part of our environment, but the color of the wallpaper is not because we have our eyes closed and can not see it. If a rock falls from a cliff and hits a person on the head, the rock is not part of that person's perceived environment until he realizes that he has been hit on the head. The perceived environment is that which we can detect.

For an organism that relies on reaction to the environment, instead of instinct, the reaction must be to adapt to the environment. The reaction to the environment must produce a special result in the organism. The reaction must cause the organism to feel good if the environment is good for it. The organism must have this special characteristic, a feeling of what is good for itself, of what allows it to survive.

A positive reaction to stimulation gives the individual a feeling of security. This feeling of security is perceived by the individual as being good for itself. Sometimes this is food. Sometimes this is sex when its genes decide it is time to reproduce. Sometimes this is a pleasant daydream. The individual reacts to the stimulation and measures that reaction in terms of security. A positive reaction gives security; a negative reaction gives insecurity. For a lion, feeling secure is being with other lions on a grassy plain with a herd of fat zebras grazing nearby. Food makes you feel secure and so does warmth in cold weather. Pleasant thoughts also make you feel secure.

Each moment in time, we react to our perceived environment. We react to what is being sensed outside our body and what we are feeling inside our body. The feeling of security we (and other organisms) have is our chemical reaction to our perceived environment at this one moment in time.

We can not just react to each moment independently of all previous and future moments and expect to survive. Fortunately, we remember and our memories can be used to find feeling-secure environments and to avoid feeling-insecure environments. The wiser, longer lasting organism has more memories and can plan further into the future.

Feeling secure is not something that can be saved up or kept in a container. But it can be used to develop habits and actions. These habits, thoughts, and actions help to create other environments to which we will react with security or insecurity.

We use our experiences to build environments where the probability of feelings of security is greatest. This is no guarantee of future security. If you have a loving spouse and a quiet home, and a good job; you could still lose the job and the spouse could die. Adapting to the environment based on feelings of security does not make us secure. It does give us a tool to try to maximize the probability of future environments that will give us a feeling of security. It is not a perfect tool, but it is all we have. It has worked well enough for us to have survived as a species, but it is no guarantee to the individual.

We are reacting to the environment as we perceive it, not as it actually is. That we have survived as a species this long says that the technique is good enough, for the species. It should be noted that like the deer running from a mountain lion and falling over a cliff, man seeks his security well enough to survive as a species; he does not necessarily seek his security perfectly.

Our ability to create security-giving environments (the loving spouse, the quiet home, the good job) is our level of security. This level of security shows itself in the environments we have developed over time and the pattern of behavior that allows us to react to increase our security over time.

Each individual reacts to the environment as he perceives it; the environment acts on each individual regardless of how he perceives it. This is a frightening confrontation. We are not aware of the future; we can not predict it. We do not know if we are about to die of a heart attack. We do not know if we will be killed this afternoon in a car accident. It is this—what we perceive the environment to be as opposed to what it may be about to do to us—that causes us concern.

We would like to know that we could tell the future in the stars or we could have our palm read and the future would be there to see. At least, if we could not control it, we would know what it is. Unfortunately, if there is one thing we know, it is that we can not predict the future and, although we can prepare for it, we can not control it. We can not perceive what is outside our environment. Yet, we know that is where the danger lies. From that unknown will come the news someone died or someone is sick or something terrible has happened. No matter how hard we wish and try, what we perceive the environment to be now is not necessarily what the real environment actually is now and will be in the future. The real environment and the perceived environment are two separate things.

What are we to do? All we can do is to act now as best we can to preserve ourselves and our species. We will follow our philosophy, our rules, our personal laws, and we will hope for the best. If our rules are good enough, we should do well. If our rules are poor, we may do badly. Maybe not all of us following good rules will do well, but that will be the trend.

There is this gap to bridge between what we perceive and what the environment really is and will be. We hope our rules will allow us to survive both as an individual and as a species. If there are natural laws of human behavior, that is what they are: rules that describe behavior patterns that allow us to make the best possible use of our environment now and in the future so that we survive both as individuals and as a species. When we speak of the accuracy of laws and theories, we are measuring whether they describe what affects and will affect human beings. This is what is relevant. The best an individual can do is to control himself, his thoughts and actions, to maximize his opportunities and chances for secure environments.

Life is too competitive to just wait for "feeling secure" environments to come to you. You have to go find them; you have to find your own food and shelter. To have survived as a species under the laws of nature, man must have something in his internal makeup that causes him to react to his environment in such a way as to seek his own individual security.

This is the first theory of security: Each individual human being seeks what he perceives to be his own individual security.

To summarize, human beings are living organisms who function by reacting to genetic and environmental stimuli in a way that is good for the individual. Human beings have had to survive in nature and the only way to do that is to react to the environment in such a way that enough individuals survive to reproduce and continue the species. Security is the feeling the organism gets when it reacts positively to its environment. Human beings act the way they do because the individual is seeking what he perceives to be his own individual security.

Chapter Three

ASSOCIATION

It is not enough to just recognize security. To survive means making decisions and this requires an ability to learn. Since man is seeking his own individual security, "learning" means recording the security in an environment.

Foxes must learn not to attack skunks, lions must learn to stalk and kill, and man must learn what plants to avoid eating. An organism whose behavior is not instinct-controlled must learn or the species will not survive.

When the individual reacts to his environment, he "learns" by forming an association with that environment. The association is a feeling of security or insecurity. Eating food makes us feel good. Early in life we form an association of security with food. We have an association of security with our favorite baseball team. We have an association of insecurity with that team losing. If we touch a hot stove, we get burned and it hurts and we develop an association of insecurity with touching a hot stove.

Associations record the security and insecurity attached to an environment, and they attach that security or insecurity to everything in the environment. It's a living room with blue chairs and a red rug. The actions that take place in that environment are recorded. We tripped over the edge of the red rug. We record our own thoughts and feelings. We remember our embarrassment and how our cute cousin laughed. We also can record facts, such as "be careful of the edge of the red rug when entering Aunt Harriet's living room". Whatever we have perceived in the environment is recorded.

An extreme example of this is superstition. For instance, if a basketball coach wears a pink jacket for the first time and his team wins, he may become superstitious about the jacket and continue to wear it. He feels an association of security with the pink jacket as part of the security he feels from the victory. A few loses will effectively counter the association and the superstition will end.

Confidence is another example of an association of security with an environment. That environment (or parts of it) have produced security in the past. For instance, you are scared on your first day of school. Later, after you have made friends and found your way around, you go with confidence.

Despair is the opposite of confidence. This is an extremely strong association of insecurity with the environment. The association is so strong that it creates an association of insecurity with all possible alternative environments. The person with tendencies toward despair must, despite his associations, change his environment or find a new one, for he is not getting enough security from his present environment.

Our associations record experiences and automatically inform us if the present environment was secure or insecure in the past. For example, if a student fails a course in school, he builds associations of insecurity with that course's environment. This includes the subject, the teacher, the classroom, and studying the subject. Twenty years later, the student may return to that school and feel insecure in that classroom. For early man to survive, he had to know whether danger or food existed in environments with certain plants, noises, smells, and sounds. Was that noise made by a fat zebra or a hungry lion?

There is a purpose to creating associations for the entire environment. An insecurity from an environment may seem to be related to one thing more than to another. However, that which appears to be the cause of an insecurity may not be the real cause. It may be something else in the environment. The "feelings" from associations are a necessary survival mechanism of the organism that learns from the environment, instead of acting from instinct.

In creating an association with the entire environment, man creates associations with specific things in the environment, including other people. Just as we associate sadness and insecurity with our own problems, so we can also feel sadness and insecurity with the problems other people have. We can recognize the joy in others at their success, just as we have felt it with our own.

Thus, associations can give us a sensitivity to others. We "feel" for others. When we see someone being sad, we tend to feel sad. This allows us to enjoy stories and movies. We feel the joy and triumphs of the characters in the story. We can also feel the joy and anticipation of weddings and the fear and sadness at funerals. Did you ever notice that in a room of small children when one starts to cry, some of the others will start crying?

Organisms that depend on behavior to survive must be sensitive to others of their kind. Each must notice when another reacts to fear or food. If he does not, he increases his chances of being eaten or starving.

Sensitivity to others allows us to be social and to fall in love. Our concern for others gives them security and causes them to associate security with us and with being sensitive. Sensitivity allows us to be a good manager and a good employee and to be aware of our customer's needs. This is not a jungle, but sensitivity is critically important to keeping a job for food and shelter and to keeping a spouse for reproduction (and a good time).

Sensitivity can result in behavior for the benefit of the group. This is the cause of behavior that is done just for the good of it. When people volunteer to help others and when they give to charity, this is their likely motivation.

We are seeking our own individual security and, when we associate that security with sensitivity to others, we create a battleground within ourselves. We have to decide every day whether to work for ourselves or the common good. Usually we realize that our individual security is the easiest thing for us to control and increasing that, increases the security of the group.

If you cause insecurity to others, your sensitivity will cause you to feel insecure as you associate with the victims of your actions. You feel bad when you remember being angry at your friend. When you remember insulting others, you remember feeling hurt when you were insulted. Causing insecurity to others is not, generally, to your advantage; because you are either causing insecurity to yourself if you are sensitive, or you are not sensitive and have lost the opportunity for the security that sensitivity can give you.

It must be noted that sensitivity is an association, not an instinct. Sensitivity gives the individual a lot of security, but it is an association that may never develop or may be overcome. When this happens, it is a costly defeat.

There are some other things to realize about associations. For instance, they do not consider the future; they record the environment at only one moment in time. Thus, if we eat food now, it will make us feel good, but later we may have a stomachache. Associations give advice; they do not necessarily show the best way.

Associations do not solve problems; they avoid them. If a person feels threatened, his associations tell him to leave the environment of the threat. However, avoidance of a source of insecurity is not always the best action. It may put off a problem and only make the avoidance more difficult or impossible in the future. Associations are one moment in time, but your time is not just one moment—it is the rest of your life.

We retain an association with an environment, not necessarily the reason for the association. Associations cause us to feel secure or insecure in a given environment without having to analyze the environment first. This was particularly helpful to early man when he walked into a dark cave and heard a strange noise. (It is better to run than be eaten.) When we are taught how to behave or to act in our society, we often ask why and are given no answer except that things are always done that way. At one time the reason was known and there developed an association of security with a certain way of doing something. The reason is lost, but the association remains. A lot of our rules of polite behavior are this way.

Associations have different strengths. They must have for us to make decisions. Spending money for gas for a car is an association of insecurity, but that car gets a person to work so he can earn money which he associates with security. If one association did not have more strength than the other, he would not have the association necessary to go to work.

The strength of an association with an environment is affected by the length of time the environment lasts. The longer the environment lasts; the stronger the association. An example of this is a student studying for a test. When he looks at a piece of information, it becomes part of his environment. The longer he looks, the stronger the association and the better the possibility that he will be able to recall it for a test. Of course, there are other factors affecting the strength of an association so that just staring at a book does not guarantee a good test grade.

We all remember that George Washington was the first president of the United States. This is not because we have studied the fact for a long time, but because of the number of occurrences of this fact in our environment. (See, it just happened again!) The number of occurrences of an environment affects the strength of the association. The greater the number of occurrences; the greater the association. For instance, the first time we drive to grandma's house, we are very uncertain of the route. The next time we do better. The third time we know the route well. This is because the association is strong enough to recall easily.

It is said that time makes things better. We feel that over time the tragedies and uncertainties of the past are wiped away. What happens is that we are recording associations constantly and more recent associations tend to have more strength than past associations. It is the associations acquired over time that remove the insecurities of the past. The insecurity caused by your favorite basketball team losing last week is replaced by the security of a big win this week.

Along this same line—that the most recent association tends to have more strength—the present environment tends to exert a strong influence. If you are daydreaming in an empty room, that room is not exerting much influence on you. However, to survive, man must be able to react to changes in that environment. If a tiger walks into the room, you stop daydreaming and react. The present (or more recent) association or environment possesses great strength.

The strength of an association is also affected by the environment in which the association exists. When we first hear a particular rock-and-roll song, we daydream of beautiful people and good times at school. This becomes the association with that particular song. There is an association of security with that song because it is in the environment with the daydream. But, the present environment can change from relaxed daydreaming to something else. The association with the song will become part of associations with a strong present environment. When that song is played in a room with yelling brothers and sisters, it begins to acquire associations with other, less secure environments. Eventually, the secure association with the daydream is replaced by the less secure one of home life and the song temporarily loses its association with security. Later, after the insecure associations have had time to weaken, the song is played in a daydreaming environment and it regains its association of security.

Connections between associations can also create new associations. If a person belongs to a local historical society, he may find that the society likes brick sidewalks due to their historical significance. Because he associates the historical society with security and the historical society associates brick sidewalks with security, this person may develop an association of security with brick sidewalks. This is a secondary association. The person has had no experience with brick sidewalks to cause him to develop an association with them.

Secondary associations can cause some problems. Although they are real associations, there is no connection between the association and any security experience the person has had. When his town proposes to replace old brick sidewalks with new cement ones, the member of the historical society may find himself opposed to the project based on the secondary association. His opinion should be based on how the project will affect his security. Are the old sidewalks unsafe so that someone falling will sue the city and thus cause taxes to rise? Or, is this an idea by a person who likes to spend money, thus raising taxes unnecessarily? Secondary associations are not necessarily relevant to your security.

An example of a secondary association is our association of security with noble deeds. We imagine these as being above the individual's own interest. Nevertheless, social rewarding of noble acts creates an association of security with those acts. (Many of our ideas about nobility were instituted by the church to control the barbarians who replaced the Roman Empire.) This means a person seeking his own security will associate security with such acts and for that reason will act in a noble manner.

Prejudice is also a secondary association. When something noticeable appears in several environments with which one associates insecurity, that aspect of the environment acquires an association of insecurity. If there is no counter to the association, a prejudice develops. (People are never prejudiced against people they like.)

Although secondary associations are not based on any security experience a person has had, they do serve a purpose. After all, we do not want to learn everything from experience. Sometimes it is better to learn from the experience of others. What a waste of time and hindrance to progress if every generation had to invent the wheel. It is by the secondary association that we learn most of our culture, by acquiring the associations of our parents and our society.

Connections between associations do not necessarily create new associations; instead, they create association chains. A thing that is recorded in one association probably exists in many associations. Its existence in these various associations links these associations together. There may be a red chair in several associations. So, when a person sees a red chair, he has a tendency to recall all the associations with red chairs in them. When we feel sad, we tend to recall other associations in which we felt sad. This connection between associations allows us to remember, to think, and to dream. This is an association chain.

Association chains can be interrupted by several things. The outside environment can interrupt the chain. For instance, the beeping of a horn may interrupt your daydream as the guy behind you reminds you that the light has turned green. You may even have associations that prevent you from proceeding further. This is when you say to yourself, "Oh, I don't want to think about that." Finally, you may have an association that is so strong that nothing can weaken it enough to have it replaced and so you can not think further. When a loved one has just died, it is very difficult to think of funeral arrangements and wills.

Dreaming is a prime example of the following of an association chain. Our most powerful associations control the dream. These are usually our most recent ones. If a person had an uneventful day and a romantic evening, he is likely to have a pleasant dream. The links between associations result in our experiencing a series of events in our dreams that are illogical. We move from one place to another without transportation. Characters enter and leave the story without our really understanding where they came from or where they are going. When we dream, we are just following an association chain.

Thinking uses association chains. Associations are linked by creating weak associations between existing associations. Thinking involves creating these associations, examining them, creating other associations, destroying associations, and creating still other associations. The associations that are created are very weak because they are of such short duration and do not have much security attached to them.

Thinking is a rejection or acceptance of associations linked with an environment and further links from those pieces of information that are accepted (second president—Thomas Jefferson—possibly, but not—maybe from New England—name starts with "A"—Adams—John Adams). This is not some magic with you trying to match some fact with the answer stored somewhere in your head. What you are doing when you are thinking is finding the strongest possible association of security for the environment you are in. There is an insecurity posed by a test question and you seek security by finding a thought with the greatest association of security. If you studied well and built a strong association with second president, John Adams, then you will answer correctly. If the strongest association you have is with Thomas Jefferson, you will answer just as confidently and be wrong. If you have no association with the answer or two associations of about equal strength, you will be confused and uncertain.

Some solutions require more than just recalling the answer that you already know. A person must be able to sift through his associations to link together a series of associations that will answer the problem. Discovering how to build a bridge in the wilderness requires a person to sort out the relevant data from all his associations. He must recall knowledge of trees, how to cut them, and how to tie knots. Perhaps, he will reject techniques of wading, swimming, and boat building.

Such thinking requires long association chains with time to construct them. The association a person has at one moment in time is part of his internal environment. Our external environment is the environment exclusive of our associations of the moment. When our senses perceive something in the external environment, our thoughts are interrupted.

You can feel secure from associations that are part of your internal environment. Thinking happy thoughts makes you feel good. That is okay and serves us well. There is a purpose to associations affecting our security. The strength of our associations is affected by our environment (external and internal). Nightmares may make us feel insecure, but they do not necessarily lower our security in the long period of time. While we sleep (or daydream) we are existing in an external environment that is secure. The associations of our nightmare are being reallocated ever so slightly with that environment. Since the events causing the association must be strong, it appears that dreaming is a built-in device for weakening strong associations that could make us feel overly secure or insecure long after the event to which we are reacting.

However, we still live in the real world and survival requires us to react to the external environment. Indeed, we are often judged by our fellow human beings based on how well we handle the real world. Are you able to provide for food, clothing, and shelter for yourself and your dependents? How well do you get along with others? How do you handle conflict?

When a person is not receiving much security from his external environment, his association of security with that environment gets weaker. He begins to get a lot of his security from his internal environment. Since his actions are related to his associations, he will begin more and more to act based on his own association chains instead of his external environment. Others will notice that he is not reacting to his external environment as most people react. They will say he is behaving irrationally.

Actually, the internal environment does not give much security. It just helps us over the rough spots. Thinking of food is just not the same as sitting down to a good meal, and thinking of friends is never as good as being with them. Receiving security from the external environment should cause the person to again react to the real world because he should have a stronger association of security with it than with his own association chains.

If a person is receiving too much insecurity from his external environment, he may internally generate an association of security with death (that, in his mind, being the alternative to the environment in which he finds himself). This association may cause the person to commit suicide.

If your environment is causing more insecurity than security, then it is poisoning you. Leave that environment, and find a better one. Perhaps your insecurity is in your own internal environment, caused by your own association chains. If so, change your associations. Recognize your insecurity and fix it by changing your environment or your associations or by acting to overcome the insecurity. Death is nothing, and anything is better than nothing. You have only one life. What harm is it to find another environment or think other thoughts or try another course of action? Try something else! You might as well have a good time while you are here. Don't quit life until it is taken from you.

Reaction to the external environment triggers associations which are weak or strong depending on the situation. The strength of these associations is the priority level of the environment. A tiger walking into your room creates a high priority level external environment. Your sister walking past your room is a low priority level, unless she suddenly screams (just to make you jump). The strength of the association with the external environment is the priority level of that environment.

Boredom occurs in an environment with a low priority level. The bored person has no strong association with that environment. For instance, if you know nothing about classical music, you may be bored at a symphony concert because you have no associations with that type of music.

Thinking requires a low priority level environment. In order to follow the association chains that thinking requires, you need minimal interruption from the external environment. The more interference there is from the external environment, the less time is available to follow and create association chains. Because the associations linking the chains are so weak, they generally need to be reconstructed after the chain is broken by the external environment. Thus we have the phrase "broken concentration", which explains why chess players get so upset at, what must seem to be, minor disturbances.

Human beings work on only one conscious level. While watching TV, listening to the radio, and reading a book; we shift rapidly among the three. As a result, we miss part of the TV program, and part of the song on the radio, and we have to go back and reread part of the book. Nevertheless, we have only one conscious level, because that is all we need, and dealing with reality is confusing enough without an added complexity.

At any one moment in time, control of the conscious level is held by the external environment or by our strongest association (internal environment). The external environment can acquire control of the conscious level through our senses. For instance, a sudden bright light, a loud noise, salty foods, cool breezes, and bad odors can all get control of the conscious level. The external environment can cause genetically-controlled reactions, such as pulling our hand back from a hot stove.

Control by the external environment is usually temporary; because, if we are not creating an association from our burned hand and the stove, we link the external environment to an association which then gives us an evaluation of the external environment for security or insecurity. This association will then link to other associations unless the external environment is strong enough to interfere once again.

The associations with the external environment are the result of learning. A child is not born with the knowledge that stoves are hot and can hurt. So, when he encounters one, no association of insecurity affects his actions. The second time he encounters a stove, he will have an association of insecurity either from his mother's warning or his experience of getting burned. This association will be strong and will probably control his conscious level and prevent him from touching the stove.

Man can control the strength of his associations by using other associations against them. Associations can be destroyed simply by thinking contrary thoughts. If you thought that Thomas Jefferson was the second president of the United States, you would have an association that you would have to destroy. This is more difficult than learning that John Adams is the second president of the United States. Just learning "John Adams—second president" is not good enough. It leaves you with two associations with about the same strength; confusion will be the result. So, you must also think "Thomas Jefferson—not second president, third president."

Unfortunately, having the right association does not necessarily guarantee the right action. How many people think, "I should not eat this" when they have a milk shake? The problem is that the action is caused by the strongest association with that environment. "I should not eat this" was not a strong enough association in that environment. There are two solutions: either the person should strengthen his association against eating milk shakes or he should avoid the environment that is going to link to the strong milk shake association. In other words, stay out of ice cream parlors. Avoid the environment where the strength of an association will cause an act that will not be the best for you over the long period of time.

Since an association is with an environment, one way to change the association is to go back to the environment and to create another association. There is an old saying that when you fall off a horse, get on him again right away. This is good advice. First, the fall causes an association of insecurity and the longer you wait to counter it, the more you will think about it and the stronger that association of insecurity will grow. Secondly, getting back on the horse puts you in an environment where you are getting security riding the horse. Falling off the horse created an association of insecurity with riding horses. Getting back on and riding creates an association of security with riding horses. This new association counters the old one and changes your association toward riding horses. (Of course, if you are not a good rider and the horse is difficult, your association is giving you good advice.)

Let us assume that you have an insecure association with going to a party. It automatically causes a chain of insecure thoughts. You will miss a show on television; you have to get dressed up; when you get there, you will have to watch your manners so that you do not do anything embarrassing; and you will spend the evening trying to make small conversation with people you do not know. The way to counter this chain of insecure thoughts is to think of a chain of secure thoughts about the party. Think of the friends who will be there. Think of the beautiful people and their clothes. Think of the free food and drink. Think that the TV show will be on and everyone can sit around and talk about it. Think how pleased your spouse (or parents) will be that you went to the party. The way to counter an insecure association backed by a chain of insecure associations is to think of a chain of secure associations. This should weaken or even destroy the insecure association that started the chain.

Can we, then, rule our environment more than it rules us? Good environment helps a person to acquire associations that will give him more security. This is because a good environment will have more time of low priority level so that the person will have more time to strengthen his associations. Man uses association chains to create associations that are not in his external environment. He goes to war to find glory. He crossed the North American continent to find gold. He studies books so that he can get an education and a better job. Associations create curiosity and desire and this causes actions that are not the result of the environment. It is man's ability to control his associations that sets him free of the limits of his environment.

You can imagine yourself spending all your time trying to create and then destroy different associations so that you can best acquire security. You would spend more time worrying about your associations than you would spend doing anything else. Furthermore, an association that seemed to work one time may not seem to work another time and you would just be left confused.

What is needed is an absolute set of associations that will provide the maximum amount of security over time in every possible situation. This is what the Natural Laws of Human Behavior must provide.

To summarize, associations are a tool for survival. By recording the security and insecurity in an environment, associations allow us to learn. The association is with everything in the environment. However, the reason for the association may not be remembered. Associations have different strengths. The strength is affected by the length of time the environment lasts, the number of occurrences of that environment, how recent the environment was, and other associations linked to that environment. There are secondary associations and association chains created by connections between associations. Associations record only one moment in time, they do not consider the future and they do not solve problems. Man works on only one conscious level. Control of the conscious level is held by the external environment or by our strongest association. (You are either thinking or reacting.) Most importantly, associations can be changed.

Associations are important because they are a person's memory, his thinking, and his feeling. Associations are the means by which man records what is security and what is not. The strongest association at any one point in time determines the person's action at that point in time, but, the relationship between association and action is not simple.

Chapter Four

ACTION

People act to gain security or avoid insecurity. Of course, there is genetically-controlled action, such as breathing and digesting food. Actions, except the genetically controlled actions, are built from associations.

Genetic dictates to action are a necessary part of man's survival. We are not aware of breathing or digesting our food. The uniqueness of genetic urges is that the action is initiated by the body itself. The body can even control the conscious level, if it is necessary. When we are hungry, we have a strong urge to eat. If we are suffocating or starving, we become aware of it very quickly with a strong association of insecurity.

Except for these genetic interferences, we act toward our environment on our conscious level. The conscious level is controlled by either an association or the external environment. Associations may have actions associated with them. If that association has control, then we perform that action. If a person has the action of dancing associated with Saturday night, when he notices it is Saturday night, he will link to that association and go dancing.

If we had no associations controlling our actions, we would act for our immediate security with no consideration for future consequences. But, we learn as we grow older that we can get into a lot of trouble if we act just for the moment, so we build associations to restrain our actions. How well we control our actions depends on the strength of the associations we have built and whether our environment links to those associations. After all, it is easier to avoid eating ice cream if you are home weighing yourself with no ice cream in the house. Your external environment (the scales) are linking to "over weight" associations. In the ice cream parlor, your external environment is linking to the "ice cream is good and will make me happy" association.

(How much security we have now and in the future depends on how well we control our actions and the quality of the associations we have developed.)

The external environment will cause an action either to seek security or to avoid insecurity. Generally, the action will be caused by an association that has been linked to by the external environment. For example, if you notice a moving car coming toward you, this links to the association that moving cars can cause insecurity, so you get out of the way.

How much do we control our actions? When we move out of the way of a moving car, it may be that we have an association against large things coming at us. Whether it is that or instinct is not clear and not important. Suffice it to say, there are actions we take quickly and do not spend time examining our associations.

There is an advantage to this type of action. No time is wasted between the moment the environment is sensed and the person acts. There is no chaining from one association to another. There is no link from one association to a contrasting association that may result in confusion and indecision. If you step in front of a moving car, you must act then. You can not take the time to think about what to do.

The disadvantage to this quick action is the same as the advantage. Failure to examine association chains means that the solution to the environment may not produce the greatest security over time. For instance, if you felt that you had been insulted, you could hit the person who insulted you. That would produce security because you would have eliminated a source of insecurity and would have gained security from associations with "acting like a man". Of course, if the person you hit was a policeman, who was not insulting you, but politely asking you to stop disturbing the peace, you are in trouble.

Proper use of quick action requires the development of some strong associations. Build contrasting associations to minimize the strength of an association triggered by an environment. You must recognize that which is really relevant to your security and that which is not. A moving car coming toward you is relevant to your security; an insult is not. Emotional action is an advantage only against a real source of immediate insecurity.

Other things we do require the development of long association chains. When we get angry, we often have developed an association chain which has left us feeling more and more threatened and insecure, until we attack the source of this association of great insecurity.

Taking the time to build association chains does not mean we will act wisely. Indeed, getting angry is generally regarded as childish behavior. As we have gotten older, we have realized that just building association chains to help us act does not necessarily give us the best results, so we have built other, strong associations to help us. The association chain is just a linking started by an external environment. Our new, strong association is a restraint against developing association chains that result in actions which benefit us for the moment, but not for the future.

We often build strong associations just to keep us acting the way we want to so that we are not distracted by the whims of our current environment. We do this by building a strong association of security with that action. The student goes to school so he can get a job and support a family. It may not be fun. It may not give security at the moment, but he knows that if he wants those things, he has to go to school and he has to study. Thinking about the security to be attained strengthens the association of security with that action. The association with the determination is also chained to other associations. The result is an action that has an extremely strong association. Although the determination will not completely control the conscious level, once a high priority level external environment has been handled, the control of the conscious level will return to the determination.

The determination does not last forever because associations change in strength. This results in changing determinations. Old ones tend to fade away temporarily or permanently. A person might watch a football game and decide to start jogging to get into shape. Then, supper is ready and he would rather eat. After supper, he is tired and would rather watch a good television program. The association of security with being able to run for a touchdown is weakened by associations from other environments. If the association were stronger, he would go running. If there is some real hope of gain, such as being 15 years old, instead of 40, then the association would tend to be stronger. Determinations are not broken (associations are); determinations are replaced.

Determination's advantage is seeking security with a goal in mind. You can use determination to help you gain security that may be hard to attain. A person using determination to guide his actions has more control over the influences of his environment, because he is aware of the security that he is trying to achieve.

Another type of action is a restraint. Restraints are actions that are such a strong part of the association they are done automatically, almost without thinking. Putting your napkin in your lap when you sit down to dinner, and saying hello and smiling when you are introduced to someone are examples of such restraints. Actions, as part of the environment, have security associated with them. Perhaps the association is the insecurity dealt out by your mother for failing to use correct table manners. Like all associations, the reason for the feeling of security or insecurity about an action is often forgotten. When we put our napkins in our laps, it is not always because we remember our mothers scolding us for not doing so. We associate that course of action with security in the environment of sitting down to eat a meal. The expected security to be gained by the action is likely forgotten or at least no longer remembered when the action is taking place.

Forming restraints takes time. Or rather, it takes time to form associations with an action attached to them. One does not form restraints; one forms associations. The restraint-association is like any other association. It can be built. It can be destroyed. If it is associated with security and the restraint in it causes insecurity, then it will be broken. A person who pets every dog he meets will stop after he gets bitten.

The restraint-association gets control of the conscious level the same as any other association. This is both an advantage and a disadvantage. The person acts almost automatically with very little time needed to control the conscious level to institute the action. The problem is that if the association does not get control of the conscious level, the action will not be taken. In the middle of a heated argument, you will sit down to dinner before the hostess is seated, you will forget your napkin, and you will forget to thank your hostess for the meal.

Restraints do not necessarily produce the security they appear to produce. As long as a restraint continues to produce some security or does not directly cause a loss of security, we will continue to keep that restraint. This may mean lost opportunities to increase our security. Perhaps we avoid people of different cultures, just because that is the way we were brought up. If so, we will miss the friendship and the knowledge of life those other cultures have.

We should periodically review our restraints. Are they maximizing our security or merely retaining it? In addition to the lost opportunity, restraints can actually cost us security. Restraint actions in one environment may give security at that moment in time, but the restraint action may result in a person being placed in an environment that causes a loss of security. Since the restraint would not be directly responsible, it would not be broken (associated with the insecurity). For instance, if a person were complimented for his nice, fashionable clothes; he could form a restraint about having new clothes. The result could be insecurity caused by financial difficulty.

Reviewing restraints requires a restraint telling you to consider the consequences of your actions and to take the action that will best increase your security. It is necessary to have restraints that allow you to take the time to examine your associations. Once a week or so, sit by yourself in a quiet place and consider what you are doing and how you are behaving toward others. Consider if this is best for you and best for them in the long run. Are you just acting from habit? Or, do you have some logical reason for your actions? With these considerations, a person can control his own actions and his environment. The alternative is to have your environment control you.

Recognize restraints. A philosophy of life is a restraint. It suggests courses of action based on logical thought. However, logical thought is merely the process of stringing together associations. If you act based on a philosophy of life, be aware that you are probably using associations to govern your actions. These associations are not necessarily going to maximize (or even increase) your security. You should review your philosophy of life just as you should review any restraint.

A person acts for two reasons. He acts to remove that with which he associates insecurity from his environment and he acts to achieve that with which he associates security.

Removing insecurity can be done by leaving the insecure environment or by attacking and destroying the cause of insecurity. If a person is unhappy in his job, he leaves it and finds another job. If he is having a disagreement with a friend, he solves the disagreement.

Insecurity from past associations deserves special comment because our attempts to remove such insecurity explain a lot of our behavior in the present. Remembering associations of insecurity make us feel insecure which causes us insecurity. A rich man seeing a slum may have his security decreased by the thoughts of the poverty which is something he has avoided and dreads. Actions taken to eliminate insecure associations by changing the environment are purges. A purge has two results; one good, one bad.

The good is that purge causes giving just for the sake of the gift. The security is gained from the giving itself. Purge is what causes people in many instances to do good, just for the sake of doing good. A church or other institution will receive gifts from someone simply because of the good the institution performs. The purge often results in anonymous gifts and anonymous deeds. The donor does not want to be bothered by people praising him for something whose reward was in the action. (Security theory is not a cynical view of man. Many people act to do good for its own sake. Remember that we act, but that does not mean we know the cause of our actions.)

Not all attempts to erase the insecurity of the past result in good deeds. Revenge is also a form of purge. Inflicting insecurity on those who have inflicted it on you is one of man's oldest characteristics. The association of insecurity is linked to those who caused it. After revenge, the link will lead to the association of security with the revenge inflicted on the original inflicters. Revenge does not have to be physical action. It can be shouted insults or just nasty thoughts.

Purge has little value. It is an action taken in response to an environment of the past. An individual's security is the result of preventing insecurity and of finding security in the present and the future. Eliminating insecurities of the past by essentially covering them up (masking them with other associations) does not solve the sources of insecurity of the present. Purge is one of man's great illusions.

An environment results in certain restraints and associations. These are used to overcome some insecurities in the external environment. Unless a person has developed certain associations toward factors in the environment, he will not react to problems in that environment until his security has been lowered. Unless you have strong associations about the rate of inflation, you will ignore it. However, when the family budget can not meet expenses, you will suddenly become greatly concerned and will then vote your congressman out of office, look for a higher paying job, etc.

There is an article on revolution by James C. Davies which appears in "Perspectives on the Social Order" by H. Laurence Ross (The American Sociological Review 27:1, 1962). Mr. Davies's theory says that rising satisfaction leads to rising expectations. When the satisfactions fail to keep rising, the expectations may continue to rise. When the gap between expectation and satisfaction gets large enough, a revolution will occur.

Eventually the environment will cause such insecurity as to destroy the restraints that caused you to vote for the same man, keep the same job, etc. Given enough time, however, the congressman and the job will establish new associations that will cause you to retain them. The congressman will blame the other party and say that in time of crisis, experience is needed. The job will say there are no other opportunities and it offers security while in another job you could get laid off.

Rebound is what happens when old restraints are broken and there are no similar ones to take their place. In such a situation, the person is actively seeking security with little in the way of restraints and associations to interfere.

There is an advantage in rebound. If restraints have indirectly caused a loss of security, rebound can break those restraints, at least temporarily.

Actions not governed by those restraints may increase your security and develop new restraints that will prevent the old ones from reasserting themselves. Perhaps a person has continued on a job out of loyalty to the company or a former boss. The job may be causing insecurity. The person may rebound, quit, and find a better job. The security from finding the best job may prevent the restraint of company loyalty from reasserting itself.

The disadvantage to destroying restraints is obvious. These actions are there because at one time they increased your security.

Every person has a level of security, and there are two aspects within that level. One is the security from a person's external environment. Money in the bank, a good job, a good spouse, and a home are all part of a person's security level. These are accumulated over time as a result of seeking security. The other aspect of a person's level of security is internal. These are the associations and restraints that have been built and strengthened over time.

Level of security is important for its potential. A person with a high level of security is not necessarily maximizing his security, and he is not necessarily very secure at any one moment in time. After all, nice people in large houses have relatives who die and have automobile accidents, etc. The potential in level of security is the potential to form associations and restraints. The higher the level of security, the greater the possibility of creating or being in a low priority environment. The greater the amount of time spent in a low priority environment, the greater the amount of time that can be spent in forming associations and restraints.

Mankind seeks security with actions. Of course, we have genetically dictated actions, such as breathing, and genetic suggestions for actions, such as those to satisfy hunger and reproduce. We also act deliberately seeking security or avoiding insecurity, with varying degrees of consideration of our associations. We have learned to control our actions by developing restraints, associations which associate certain actions with security and certain other actions with insecurity. Be aware of these associations and their attached actions. They can be misleading by indirectly causing insecurity or by giving security, but not the maximum security you could have had.

What are our sources of security and what is their affect on our associations and actions?

Chapter Five

SOURCES OF SECURITY

An association, in recording the security of an environment, records the source of security. This may be your mother giving you a kind word, friends congratulating you for an achievement, a hug from a special friend, a quiet walk in the evening, or the joy of a movie with a happy ending. Sources of security tend to develop strong associations of security toward them. These strong associations mean sources of security exercise a strong influence on us through secondary associations and their affect on association chains.

One obvious source of security is our standard of living; our material possessions. Food, shelter, and clothing provide us with the necessities to satisfy our genetic needs to stay alive. Having this security is important, because without it the genetic necessities would tend to control our conscious level. We would not have much time for altering associations and building restraints to control our actions and our long term gain of security would be slight.

Proper food and comfort tend to result in less sickness, thus avoiding insecurity. Transportation allows us to live in the quiet of the country (noise causes insecurity) and to work in the city. Money allows us to purchase insurance, thus avoiding worries about threats to our finances.

We also get security from accomplishments. Taking a walk makes us feel better. Getting a household chore accomplished gives us a feeling of relief and satisfaction. The things we do at work give us a feeling of security. Security of accomplishment is actually security from several different sources, some of them acting at the same time.

Because we are living organisms, there is security to be gained just from physical exercise. When we exercise, we use our muscles and strengthen them. We feel better.

Removing sources of insecurity from the external environment is also part of the security of accomplishment. Fixing a leaky roof ends a source of insecurity. Taking a walk down a quiet street removes ourselves from the insecure noise and confusion of an alternate environment.

Part of the security of accomplishment is the security received from the accomplishment. The paycheck at the end of the week gives security with the food it buys, the shelter it pays for, and the entertainment that it can buy. You have steak for dinner and a nice car because you spent eight hours a day at the office. Without that work, the security would not be there.

Our associations with accomplishments cause us to link to these associations of security, giving us more security. Great sports stars receive much adoration from other people. The president of the company has respect. When we make an accomplishment, our association linkages bring forward these associations of security. This increases our security from this accomplishment. A person playing golf may not hit a great shot, but if he beats the person he is playing with or betters his past score, he has accomplished something.

We do not always get the same amount of security from an accomplishment, particularly when it is repeated frequently. After all, the fun of doing the same thing on the assembly line disappears quickly. The accomplishment picks up other associations from the environment, and when anticipated security is not forthcoming from each accomplishment, its association of security weakens. If the result of the accomplishment is fatigue and lost opportunity, such as mowing lawns instead of going dancing, the result may be insecurity. Time away from the work can allow the associations to strengthen as ideas, such as the money to be earned, replace the fatigue and boredom.

Another source of security is the people around us. Humans tend to form groups. We enjoy the company of our friends. They support us, give us joy and relaxation, and tend to prevent us from thinking of associations of insecurity.

Each group we belong to is a society, and each society has its own set of knowledge and rules. The knowledge and rules are the society's culture. Culture is the books you read, the songs you sing, and the knowledge you use to repair your car. Culture is also the rules of acceptable behavior in that society.

Some rules are written, such as our laws. Other rules are not written, but are taught by the group. The society's rules are the result of the seeking of security by past generations. They may be the work of philosophers or great leaders who acted in ways that created an association of security with certain actions, or they may be the result of many individuals learning to adapt to their environment.

The culture must be taught to new members of the society (generally children) if the society is to continue to exist. Children are taught "good manners" and are brought up in their parent's church and political party. They are taught in schools: Reading, writing, and arithmetic are part of our culture. At home they are taught how they are to behave. The teaching is done by creating associations of security with the group and associations of insecurity with contrary actions. Children are punished for not "behaving". They are praised for using a napkin and the correct fork. They are punished for throwing food at the table.

The result of all this is that we are possessors of many associations about which we really know nothing. Our culture is imposed upon us. This is not necessarily bad. We know better how to seek our security than we could ever know if we had no culture, but we must realize that it can be improved upon. After all, our culture is an improvement upon previous cultures of previous generations.

Culture is not changed by society, but by individuals influencing society. Only by doing something that is not in the culture can something new be discovered. After all, if it is new, it is not in the culture or it would not be new. If all individuals belonged completely to society, it would never change. Only in difference is there the potential for change.

Although society may have a strong effect on us, it is only one source of security. The associations that it forms must compete with the others that we have formed. The result of this is that we are not exactly the way that society would like us to be.

Just as the society has a certain amount of power over the individual, he has a degree of power over the society. Society is only a number of individuals, each seeking what they perceive to be their own security. An individual's power in the society is determined by the amount of security associated with him by the members of the society as opposed to the amount of security they associate with the rules of the society. In a family group, the head of household has a great deal of influence. However, the same person will have little influence where he works if he is just one of many in his position and there are many persons in higher jobs.

A person's influence will be greater if there are fewer members in the group. Each group member has a certain amount of security associated with him because he is part of the security that the members of the group get from the group. The smaller the group, the greater the percentage of the group's security is available, potentially, to each member. Of course, each member will have a different amount of security associated with him simply because we all tend to act in different ways. Additionally, a person's influence is affected by the society's association with that person's position in the society. For example, a Senator has more security associated with his position than a used car salesman has associated with his.

There are times when the individual will not follow the rules of society. For example, there are students who study even though their friends get bad grades. If a rule causes a person to lose security, he may associate it with insecurity. If a child's parents cause him insecurity for doing the mischievous things his friends do, he may stop following the rules of his friends. In addition, the individual may have developed associations that result in actions that are not approved by society. What happens when the child of doctors decides to be an artist?

The rules of society that are most frequently broken are those, logically, that are the weakest. The weakest rules are those that are new and those that apply to non-group actions. New rules are not as strongly associated with the group as the old rules are. There may be members of the group who are opposed to the new rules. The associations of the members toward the member opposed to the new rule works against the building of an association of security with the new rule. Society's rules that apply to the actions of the individual when he is not in the group must be very weak. The group does not know what the individual is doing and the individual knows this.

As humanity learns new ways of seeking its own security, the rules must change. Society is like a ship on the sea headed toward the promised land of maximum security. The ship is society's rules. The sea is all possible actions. The actions of individuals leave the ship in all directions. They try to pull the ship by their example and by their logic. Sometimes society hesitates, pulled backward toward insecurity. Eventually the pull toward insecurity is severed by the associations of insecurity. Sometimes the ship may be pulled to the side, but only temporarily. Only the pulls leading forward to greater security are allowed to move society forward past old associations to new ones.

It is easy to say that we should learn from our culture and then go the best way. It is not easy to do. Actions that are contrary to those of the group are associated with insecurity and may be interpreted as a threat to the group. Persons who go to the country club and play golf tend to look on the poor who play basketball in the streets with insecurity and vice versa. The source of insecurity may be ignored or forced out of the group or destroyed. A partygoer who becomes drunk and acts friendly and speaks loudly is simply ignored. If he becomes too loud or too friendly, he is asked to leave. Should he become excessively violent and even kill someone, the police will be called and he may be killed. Society enforces its rules.

The associations that we have built with society affect our actions and the only way to act differently is to build stronger associations. This is not easy. Just how strong the associations with society can be are indicated by the following experiment. *Perspectives on the Social Order* (H. Laurence Ross, McGraw-Hill, 1963) contains an article from the Scientific American (193:5, 1955). It is "Opinions and Social Pressure" by Solomon E. Asch. It reports an experiment to test the effect on a person when he is opposed by an absolute majority. The person is one of a group which is to publicly state what they see when shown lines of varying lengths. Every person, except one, has been instructed to give the same wrong answer at various times. Even though the subject can see everyone else is wrong, the power of society is such that in about one-third of the cases, the subject is intimidated into agreeing with the others in the group.

Actually, the influence of society on the individual is not as all-encompassing as this may seem because a person actually belongs to many societies. Each group to which we belong tends to be a society. Our immediate family is a society. Our friends form another society. Our school and business associates are another. We also belong to the society that reaches us by mass communication. Our language tends to mark the range of a society. We have all read Shakespeare. We all hear the same news broadcasts and read similar things in our newspapers. Each society to which we belong is a source of security.

Moreover, each society to which we belong has its own set of rules. Since the societies are different, the rules may be different and may even be in conflict. Of course, some of those rules will be the same. You eat with a knife and fork at home, just the same as at a business lunch. But, you do not wear a tie and coat at home. The environment the person is in triggers the link to the associations with the rules of that society. However, trying to follow the rules of different societies depending on the person's environment can cause conflict within the person himself. A strong association caused by one society may cause a person to feel insecure when in the environment (rules) of another society.

Relationships between individuals are not the same as the relationship between an individual and a group. When there is a strong association in one individual toward another, society's associations will have less affect because of the strength of the association with the individual. In a strong relationship between individuals, there are no rules such as society's rules. (Of course, the individuals will tend to act within the rules of society.) There are not the rewards associated with society's approval of a person's actions. In a relationship between individuals, the rules and rewards are developed and kept by the interaction between the individuals. The interaction is a series of associations within each person.

The association that one person has for the other follows the rules of every other association. It takes time to develop strength. There must be more associations of security than insecurity. The stronger the associations of security, the better.

You must distinguish between a strong feeling of security toward a person at one moment in time and a strong association. The strong feeling is likely to be an association chain triggered by the environment and it will be broken when the environment changes. Young ladies get seduced on quiet, peaceful nights when they are feeling lonely and their only source of security is the man they are with. Of course, such conditions can also be used to strengthen an association of security.

Beware of the affect of the secondary association. You may associate security with a beautiful woman or a handsome athlete. When you come in contact with such a person, there is immediately a strong association of security with that person. It is caused by a secondary association. The image brings forth the association, not the person. This is a strong association that will last until the person who fits the image begins to acquire an association of their own.

There is a test to determine if an association is a strong association or just a temporary, strong feeling caused by an association chain run amuck. Test the association in an environment with other sources of security. At a party with other friends or while accomplishing something with which you associate security, have your friend there. If the feeling does not weaken much and if an association of security remains, then it is a strong association. If the association becomes weak or confused or even turns to insecurity, then it is not strong.

A relationship between individuals begins with the first exchanges of security between them. This creates an association of security with the other person. This source of security, like every other source, affects a person's actions. People may start doing things together. A boy and a girl may start seeing more of one another. The most important factor in developing a relationship is the amount of security a person receives from the other. This depends on the amount the other person gives, which depends on the amount he receives from the first person. There must be that exchange of security. A strong association develops into friendship; an even stronger association becomes love.

The secondary associations are important in starting the relationship. They are of less importance in keeping the relationship strong. For instance, in a relationship between a man and a woman, it is important that each appear attractive and friendly toward the other. After they are married, there will be times when the woman will have curlers in her hair and the man will come in all dirty from working on his car.

The security that one person gives must be what the other person associates with security. A man sending flowers to a woman who does not know him will not develop a relationship between the two of them. She may associate security with flowers, but she probably associates insecurity with flowers from strangers. In any case, she is developing a relationship with the flowers, not with the man.

The actions and associations developed toward the relationship are critical to its strength and duration. If the actions are taken to reach a particular goal, such as sex or marriage, once the goal is reached there will no longer be such a strong association of security with that action and it will occur less frequently. You will be giving less security to the other person, so you will not be as strong a source of security to them. A weakened relationship will be the result. For instance, a man may take a woman to nice places for dinner while they are dating. If he does that so she will marry him; after they are married, he will stop taking her out. She will no longer receive that security and associate it with him. On the other hand, if the actions and associations are developed for the security they give the other person, the strength of the relationship should continue to grow. And, the couple will continue to go to nice places for dinner.

A man and a woman falling in love and getting married often wonder if they are really in love. There seems to be a feeling in our society that if you are really in love when you get married, you will have a happy marriage. Unfortunately, this is not completely true. The security you receive depends on the other person's associations of security with you. This forces you to be sensitive to their security. If you are not, it will cost you security, and perhaps your marriage.

Weakening of an interpersonal relationship occurs when one person stops receiving security from the other. The strong association between the couple begins to weaken, and other sources of security exert their influence. The husband may spend more time bowling with the guys and she may spend more time talking with her girl friends. For each, this will weaken the other as a source of security. For each, their actions will continue to result in their finding more security elsewhere. The association that each has for the other will eventually weaken and the marriage will end.

The solution to this problem is simple. Each must consciously give the other person security. Each must realize what associations and actions he has to have and work to maintain them. Each must work to maintain that strong association of security with the other and to maintain the other's association with them.

Unlike love and marriage, not all sources of security give security for the long term. A negative security is a source of security that gives a great deal of security at any one moment in time but results in a lowering of a person's security in the future. Furthermore, the negative security takes time that would be better spent in actions that would provide more security. Because an association records only one moment in time, the lost opportunity or future insecurity caused by the negative security may not be recorded with the negative security. The negative security becomes a source of security and an influence over future actions. Negative security is a great illusion. It provides great security for the present, but it costs security later.

Alcohol is a good example of a negative security. There is presumably a great deal of security in being drunk. The drunk feels good. He no longer has associations of insecurity on a high level of consciousness. His problems are forgotten. He feels secure, but while he is drunk, he is not solving any of his sources of insecurity. If you are overweight, milk shakes can be a negative security. The negative security lures you into a world where there is no time but the present. Eventually the future comes and the security of the present is gone.

Getting rid of a source of security is not very easy. But, it is often critical to improving your actions so that you can tend to maximize your security. Just saying that you are going to change does very little to change you. You must change your associations and thereby change your actions. New sources of security must be found to replace old ones, and the new sources require time to build strong associations.

Another source of security is your own philosophy and beliefs. When following your philosophy and beliefs results in security, you associate that security to your beliefs, thus strengthening them further. Your philosophy is what you use, because it is a strong association, to control your associations and actions. If your philosophy is a strong source of security and, thus, a strong association, it is very difficult to change.

We have many sources of security. We have our standard of living, accomplishments, our own sensitivity to others, the groups we belong to, good friends, a spouse who loves us, and our own beliefs. Be aware that sources of security give us security for the moment and that may not be the same as security for the long term. Be especially aware of sources of security that give security now, but cause insecurity later.

Chapter Six

SECOND THEORY OF SECURITY

The first theory of security is that each individual human being seeks what he perceives to be his own individual security. Logically, if this is what we are and this is the way we were made, isn't this what we should be doing? After all, what-we-are has allowed us to survive as a species for all these years, and it has made us the dominant species on the planet. Shouldn't our actions be to do this best? Shouldn't we continue on, each individual trying to follow the collective actions that have done so much for the species?

A feeling of security is the result of the individual's chemical reaction to his perceived environment at one moment in time. This happens continually. Each moment giving us another reaction, making us feel secure or insecure. Fortunately, the environment we perceive is not always our external environment. Sometimes it is our internal environment. We exercise control by recording our reaction to our environment as an association and by using our internal environment to search these associations to determine the best action to take. We can do more than just record our external environment. We can record our internal environment also, developing new associations from association strings and strengthening associations. This gives us the ability to control how we react to our perceived environment.

The control we try to create in our internal environment, on how we react to our perceived environment, may be called our philosophy of life. (Of course, we do not always have the time and priority to use this philosophical control.) Some of us react to the perceived environment by getting the maximum security available at this moment in time. Others will react by taking the action which will get security in the future. It is like the grasshopper who plays all summer and starves in the winter, and the ant who works all summer and eats well in the winter.

Should we try to maximize our security over time or just have fun now? After all we could die tomorrow. Of course, what happens if we don't? Whether you go to the movies this evening or study is a decision for you to make. You need a break from studying sometime. In many respects, that is a question of finance and you can make whatever decision you wish. Decisions you make on your future have no direct effect on anything but your future security.

Can you insult someone and hurt them now just to make yourself feel better, even though over the long term it would be better to be nice to everyone? This is an option you do not have. Because you must have associations with others to maximize your security at any time, any harm you do to others will create associations of insecurity within yourself, which is not maximizing your security.

Can we do both? Can we have fun and seek security over time? Although we live in one moment of time and record our security at one moment in time, we live over many moments in time. We do not live for just a moment, and it is a hard thing to understand, but the way you live in this moment affects the environment in which you will find yourself in future moments. If you do not study now and get your degree, your future moments will have fewer material benefits and probably less security. The security you have now is the result of actions you have taken and associations you have developed in past environments. To have the opportunity to have fun now depends on past actions and associations. To have fun in the future depends on those past actions and associations plus the actions and associations of the present. You can have security now and in the future, but you have to plan. Planning means seeking your security over time.

Having fun means what? It means a low stress environment with money for food and drink. It means having friends to do things with. This requires your having gone to school or developed a skill which is valuable. It means being nice to, at least some, people most of the time. Doing these things means you took time to work at studying and training. It means you took the time to develop associations and restraints necessary to be nice to people. So, you had to seek security "over time" to get to this place. As you look back, you probably regret the actions and associations that did not increase your security "over time". You probably wish you had worked harder for your future by studying harder and by learning to not speak so quickly the things you felt, but should not have said.

(Don't worry about it. This is true for everyone who cares to remember. Do not make yourself insecure thinking about it.)

The second theory of security is that each individual should seek to maximize his own security over time. Security for the individual is better than insecurity and more security is better than less. The individual can do things to control the security he has; we are not the slaves of the happenstance of our environment. The individual can seek to maximize his security.

As we live from day-to-day, we develop certain associations and actions as we react to our environment, trying to adapt to gain security. This means our associations and actions tend to be forced on us by our environment. If this is so, we can gain security only as our perceptions to our environment teach us to adapt. Our environment teaches us to adapt to that environment—the environment we perceive, not the real environment.

How can you maximize your security by trying to adapt to the environment that you perceive? Maximizing security means adapting to the real environment over time. Maximizing security means controlling your associations and actions. It means developing within yourself the associations and actions designed to maximize your security. It means strengthening those associations and actions in yourself without waiting for your environment to give you such a jolt of security or insecurity that it does it (and does it wrong) for you.

We can learn and we can strengthen some associations so that we begin to act differently. The opportunity is given to each person to force the issue and to try to manipulate the environment to his advantage. The point is that we can strengthen and weaken our associations and thereby control our actions. We can read and listen and learn and we can use what we learn to guide us in changing the strengths of our associations. This is our great power. This is our great gift as human beings. We can control ourselves because we are not limited by the associations and their strengths as imposed on us by our external environment. We can control; we can seek to maximize our security over time.

The Second Theory of Security is that man should seek to maximize his own security over time. Since, according to the first theory, the individual seeks his security and this has allowed man as a species to survive; logically, more security should allow the individual to increase his chances of survival and to survive better. This is the analogy with the first theory. The new law proposed by this theory is that the individual should seek to maximize his security over time.

The associations and actions we should try to develop within ourselves to maximize our individual security over time are the Natural Laws of Human Behavior.

Chapter Seven

THIRD THEORY OF SECURITY

Suppose there are Natural Laws of Human Behavior which describe behavior patterns that allow us to make the best possible use of our environment now and in the future so that we survive both as individuals and as a species. These Laws tell us how to maximize our security over time. As we have discussed earlier, our own associations cloud our perceptions so we can not discover these laws ourselves, even though the security they give would make it possible to develop favorable associations toward them. As discussed earlier, if the Creator of the universe wished us to have these Laws, he would have to give them to us. If he has given them to us, they would probably be in a religion. Suppose these Laws are in the teachings of Jesus Christ.

This book will use security theory to look at the teachings of Jesus Christ to see if they contain the Natural Laws of Human Behavior. This brings us to the third theory of security: Jesus Christ gave mankind the Natural Laws of Human Behavior and only by following those laws can the individual maximize his security over time. Natural Laws of Human Behavior, as mentioned earlier, are not rules we must follow. They are rules that, if followed, maximize the probability of our survival as an individual and as a species.

If Jesus really gave mankind the Natural Laws of Human Behavior and security theory is correct, there should be some reference to these things, however obscure, in His teachings.

One of the most startling things about security theory is its reliance on the individual; to know what gives himself security. Jesus said, "Always treat others as you would like them to treat you: that is the Law and the prophets." (Matt.7:12) If Jesus wanted man to act in some non-human, non-security way; He would not have told man to treat others with what man himself associated with a secure way to be treated. Jesus is relying on the individual to determine for himself what gives security.

Jesus makes an oblique reference to natural laws when he said, "so long as heaven and earth endure, not a letter, not a stroke, will disappear from the law until all that must happen has happened." (Matt.5:18)

If Jesus wanted man to maximize his security, then He would have come to make life better for us. He should mention that somewhere, or at least hint at it. Jesus said, "Therefore I bid you put away anxious thoughts about food and drink to keep you alive, and clothes to cover your body... Set your mind on God's kingdom and his justice before everything else, and all the rest will come to you as well." (Matt.6:25-34) This is the great promise that Jesus gives man. He will give us security if we follow his laws. Jesus is not talking about some after-life happiness. He is talking about here and now; about food for the dinner table and clothes for school.

Nevertheless, most of us think of Christianity as something that is hard for us. This is confusing the necessity of forming associations and restraints with the results derived from them. Although there are many courses of action available, there is only one that will maximize your security. The correct action will be difficult, in a security sense, to take.

Is this what we are intended to do? Is this the perfection that God put in us? If God is perfect, why did He make man so imperfect? This is a nice theological question. The answer is that man is perfect. A salt shaker is a very imperfect car engine, but it is a perfect salt dispenser. Man may not be a perfect angel, but he is perfect for what God wanted him to be. If God had wanted man to be a perfect Christian, He would have made man that way and we would not have all this conflict in ourselves and in our lives.

Man has within himself the ability to develop to be what God hopes that he will become.

For some irrelevant reason, God wishes to persuade us to follow Him, not to overpower us. To each individual is given the opportunity to choose. If God did something really spectacular, we would know He was God and choosing would be easy. There would be one church and one dictated set of beliefs by that church, and God would not have achieved the individual-interpretation oriented, individual-action oriented religion that Christianity is today. Perhaps the individual needs to be persuaded and to choose to build his associations toward God so that the rules have strong associations and guide his actions.

If two theories appear to be accurate, the one with the greatest scope will be the accurate theory. No matter how accurate Jesus' rules may appear to be, another theory with greater scope would replace it. Therefore, Jesus must have a theory of universal scope.

For the scope of Jesus' theory to be universal, it must cover everything that is relevant to man. Relevance refers to those things that affect or will affect man. We are affected now by our environment; we will be affected by our future environments.

Our environment consists of man and nature. Nature is easy to handle and understand; Jesus has little to say about it. His most important comment is "seek and ye shall find". (Matt.7:7) This is a description of the scientific method which man has used this quite effectively to deal with nature.

Man is the difficult part of our environment of man and nature. Most of Jesus' laws refer to the conflict between men and our conflict within ourselves.

Since the actions of one person can affect the security of others, many people think there is a pattern to these interrelationships. These people try to play the pattern. They study the actions of others, trying to learn the pattern. They react to the actions of others. They expect other people to react in a certain way to their actions. People who play the pattern, lose. They can not maximize their security. Those who play the pattern end up following traditional rules and ideas as their culture believes those rules to be. People who follow the laws of God do not follow the pattern. Those people who are trying to learn how to act by following the pattern are looking for laws they can not find. They are looking for something that does not exist.

For a law to be accurate, it must show an invariable association between events or properties about which there is universal agreement and it must do this in the real environment. For universal scope, all God's laws must work together to give maximum probability for the survival of the species and, secondly, maximum security over time for the individual and it must do so for all possible situations. Our genetic makeup, hormones and natural urges, has been built in to take care of the survival of the species. That does not seem to be our problem at this writing.

To maximize the security of the individual over time, Jesus gave us laws that allow us to create strong associations of security with His laws so that the ultimate reward is seen only after death, thus preventing our restraints from being broken by success or failure in life. Also, there are laws to protect us against attempts to alter our associations with God's laws. There are rewards to the individual for following those laws. We are guaranteed food and drink to strengthen our associations with His laws. In addition, His laws build within us a pattern of associations that provide us with what to say and do in a crisis. We have rules that urge us to be perfect and keep us away from associations (do not mourn the dead) and actions (do not work on the sabbath) that may prevent us from maximizing our security. We have rules that allow us to learn from others and we have rules that allow us to build proper associations toward others so that we can deal with them in any situation.

We have rules for dealing with violence that allow us to avoid appearing as a source of insecurity to those who would harm us. This creates within them an association of security toward us. We have rules to deal with groups by avoiding the associations they try to create in us that would not maximize our security. We have rules that tell us to influence the group and to develop associations in them that would maximize their security. Then we have rules that warn us of the group responsibility for actions and rules that tell us to get out of the group if it can not be controlled. We have rules that teach us to be nice to others, creating associations of security in them toward us and giving us security through our sensitivity to the security of others. We have rules that tell us not to harm others. Thus, we do not create associations of insecurity toward ourselves. We have rules for dealing with sex that will maximize our security by preventing associations toward sex that would hurt our ability to get the maximum benefit from this source of security. Finally, we have rules that cause us to be a positive influence toward our fellow man; to be a peacemaker and to see right prevail thus increasing our security along with everyone else's.

In God's design of the universe and mankind and the natural laws of human behavior, there had to have been some consideration of when to use which laws. All the laws of physics work together. They may not be simple and it is sometimes not apparent which law is working. (If gravity brings everything together, why is the universe expanding?) Electrons and protons do not carry a handbook with them so they know when to act in such and such a manner. So too, the Creator of mankind had to build into us the characteristics to behave properly, if we have the associations to follow His laws. (The difference between humans and protons seems to be that we have a choice.)

Jesus says there are two great commandments and that is all He says about which associations should have the greatest strength. Jesus gives no priority to one of His laws above any other. Indeed, the laws must mesh together. Priority will come. This is what Jesus means when He says that in time of crisis we do not have to think what to say, God will give us the words to say (and the automatic actions to take).

If Jesus gave us the Natural Laws of Human Behavior, his laws must be accurate and the scope of those laws must be universal. They must cover every possible situation, giving the individual the maximum security over time he can get from his starting environment and allowing the species to survive.

So, what are these Natural Laws of Human Behavior and do they really maximize our security over time?

Chapter 8

RULES OF GOD
STRENGTHENING THE INDIVIDUAL

There is nothing in the Bible listing the Natural Laws of Human Behavior. There are, nevertheless, rules that Jesus stated clearly. These and the ten commandments, I am presuming to be the Natural Laws. Although Jesus also spoke in parables (illustrating stories whose meaning is not necessarily clear), I see nothing in the stories that would be contrary to the clearly stated laws. After all, if God is going to this much trouble, he might as well make the rules clear.

Jesus said, "Thou shalt love the Lord thy God with all thy heart, and with all thy soul, and with all thy mind. This is the first and great commandment. And the second is like unto it. Thou shalt love thy neighbor as thyself. On these two commandments hang all the law and the prophets." (Matt.22:37-40) I am dividing the discussion of laws into two parts. This chapter will discuss the laws the individual must build within himself to prepare himself for following the rules on how to interact with others.

BUILD ASSOCIATIONS WITH GOD

The Natural Laws of Human Behavior are behavior patterns. They require strong associations, so the individual will think and act according to the laws. Following the Natural Laws of Human Behavior requires very strong associations of security with these laws. So, how do you build the strong associations? First, you must have a strong association with building the strong associations.

If the ultimate goal, the security to be gained that is associated with an action, is something that we do not expect to gain during our life, but will reward us later; we have the association that will last us through the insecurities of our present and future environment. This is the reward the Christian expects for his good deeds. After he dies, the good person expects to go to heaven and rest with God for all eternity. This is the promise most religions (and some political parties) give to try to keep individuals following their ideas regardless of the security the individual receives. Whether this is considered a necessary influencing idea or the most real, important part of Christianity, it is necessary to build strong enough associations to get maximum benefits from the laws of Jesus. The following laws relate to this:

LOVE GOD. (Matt.22:37-40)
WORSHIP AND SERVE ONLY GOD. (Matt.4:10)
DO THE WILL OF GOD. (Matt.7:21-23)
CALL NO MAN YOUR FATHER ON EARTH. (Matt.23:9)
DO NOT SWEAR. (Matt.5:34-37)
DO NOT DENY JESUS. (Luke12:9)
DO NOT SPEAK AGAINST THE HOLY GHOST. (Matt.12:32)

We have so many things influencing us, so many sources of security, and they all create associations. It is easy to get distracted, and form associations that are contrary to the teachings of Jesus. This is why we should "love God" and "worship and serve only God". Swearing will create a small association of God with an insecure moment. If God's laws are absolute and difficult to follow, we need all the help we can get. Creating bad associations within ourselves is not helpful.

Your own family and its culture can be a strong influence on your associations, but there can be no associations toward one's relatives and their culture that conflict with the associations needed to follow God's laws.

RESIST ATTEMPTS TO ALTER YOUR ASSOCIATION WITH GOD

We develop a lot of strong associations in our lives. When two of these associations come against each other, we get confused. The obvious way to solve this is to create a new association of security. Since the confusion is an insecure state, we will associate the confusing parts with insecurity and associate security with those parts of the two associations that were not in conflict. When our culture has rules contrary to those of Jesus, there is strong pressure to alter His laws for our convenience. Needless to say, the Natural Laws of Human Behavior warn against this. The following laws relate to this:

HAVE NO OTHER GODS.
One of the ten commandments is,
"Thou shalt have no other gods before me."(Exod.20:3)
HAVE NO IDOLS. (Exod.20:4-5)
DO NOT TAKE THE NAME OF GOD IN VAIN. (Exod.20:7)
GIVE ALMS TO GOD IN SECRET. (Matt.6:1)
FAST IN PRIVATE. (Matt.6:17-18)
PRAY IN PRIVATE.
Jesus said, "... when thou prayest, enter into thy closet, and when thou hast shut thy door, pray to thy Father which is in secret; ...".
(Matt.6:6)

Jesus said, "If your right eye leads you astray, tear it out and fling it away; it is better for you to lose one part of your body than for the whole of it to be thrown into hell." (Matt.5:29) If a strong association leads you to unchristian actions, you must discard that association by using determination and counter associations, even if you feel as much security from that association as from your right eye.

We have lots of associations with lots of things and the strengths of those associations affect our actions. The strongest association dictates the action. The "other gods" does not necessarily refer to other religions. It refers to any association that is stronger than associations you have with God and His laws. It means following any rules that are contrary to God's. For instance, society's rules are not necessarily the same as God's. God and His laws must be your strongest associations. If you give to the church or fast or pray so that people will see you, your association of security is with society; other people seeing you act religiously so they will associate you with security. If you give and fast and pray in secret, your association of security is with God.

REWARDS TO THE INDIVIDUAL

There needs to be security gained by having the association to form strong associations with God. The security reinforces the association to develop strong associations with God. The following laws relate to this:

DO NOT WORRY ABOUT FOOD OR DRINK. Jesus said, "...
Take no thought for ..., what ye shall eat, or what ye shall drink ...".
(Matt.6:25)
TAKE NO THOUGHT OF WHAT TO SAY. Jesus said, "But when they deliver you up, take no thought how or what ye shall speak: for it shall be given you in that same hour what ye shall speak."
(Matt.10:19)
ASK AND YOU WILL RECEIVE. Jesus said, "Ask, and it shall be given you; ...". (Matt.7:7)

SEEK AND YOU WILL FIND. Jesus said, "... seek, and ye shall find; ...". (Matt.7:7)

God will provide you with food and drink. In maximizing your security, you also give security to others and they will associate you with security. You will be valuable to them and you will be paid accordingly.

Following the teachings of Jesus will develop such strong associations with His laws that not even the insecurity of the moment will interfere with those restraints. Your pattern of behavior will be strongly set and will guide you through the tough spots. So, you will speak as you should, even in the most insecure moments. Later, you may wonder why you said that, but you will have maximized your security.

Asking is associating God with security. If you do that, you will be able to follow His laws and you will maximize your security. If you ask for a television set, you may not get it. But, if you associate God with security, you will develop the restraints that make you valuable to your fellow man. Then, you will earn the money to buy the television.

The idea "ask and you shall receive" is also an area of mystery. Jesus does not say much about it. How it works is not for us to know: we must consider it to be irrelevant. If you ask for a television, you may get it. However, whether you get it should not be considered proof or disproof of the existence of God.

"Seek and ye shall find" is an endorsement of knowledge. Too often we say there are things that people should not know. If you have a behavior pattern that follows God's laws, you have the ultimate associations. Knowledge will not create contrary associations within you. Knowledge is information about the universe. God made this. You can misuse it; there are such things as negative securities, but you have God's laws which tell you how to act and, therefore, how to use knowledge. In of itself the universe is good.

RULES TO SEEK MAXIMUM SECURITY

Having a strong association toward building associations toward God, being aware of associations that might try to compromise your associations with God's laws, and knowing that you are getting security from God's laws are just the beginning. You need to develop associations to use the laws to maximize your security. You need to develop an aggressive attitude toward life. The following laws relate to this:

DO NOT TEMPT GOD. Jesus said, "... thou shalt not tempt the Lord thy God." (Matt.4:7)

ALWAYS BE READY FOR GOD. Jesus said, "... the Son of Man cometh at an hour when ye think not." (Luke12:40)

DO NOT COVET ANYTHING THAT IS YOUR NEIGHBOR'S. (Exod.20:17)

DO NOT MOURN THE DEAD. Jesus said, "Let the dead bury their dead ...". (Luke9:60)

GET MARRIED IF YOU ARE READY FOR IT. Jesus said, "That (marriage) is something which not everyone can accept, but only those for whom God has appointed it. For while some are incapable of marriage because they were born so, or were made so by men, there are others who have themselves renounced marriage for the sake of the kingdom of Heaven. Let those accept it who can." (Matt.19:11-12)

DO NOT WORK ON THE SABBATH. (Exod.20:10)

BE PURE IN HEART. (Matt.5:8)

BE PERFECT. (Matt.5:28)

Seeking to maximize your security is hard. It is so easy to avoid working on your associations and restraints. It is so easy to avoid evaluating your actions and associations as they relate to God's laws. Wouldn't it be a lot easier to just assume that God will look out for us? The act of tempting God requires an association of security with such an act, an action against God by questioning Him. (It is obvious that God is not willing to force his presence upon mankind.) The real manifestation of God is within yourself; the security you receive from following His laws.

If we can't let God do it, can we put it off until tomorrow? Many sins are such strong sources of security that even though we know God's laws will maximize our security, we may not make the effort to give up old actions because of our associations with them. Delaying the decision to follow God costs you security and gains you nothing. We may feel we can change later; Jesus says you can not expect later to be there.

Maximizing security means acquiring security. Unfortunately, that with which you associate security may not be that which maximizes your security. Covet means to desire something strongly. Jesus said, "Take heed, and beware of covetousness: for a man's life consisteth not in the abundance of the things which he possesseth." (Luke12:15) From the verse in Luke, there are really two points here. One is that you should not desire strongly something that someone else has. The other is that you should not associate security too strongly with material goods.

We tend to associate a lot of security with material things, particularly money. We get a lot of security from our standard of living, but it is by no means the only security there is for us. There is the love of others, the respect of society, power to influence others, security from accomplishment, and the inner peace that comes from following God. However, even knowing this, we tend to let material possessions become such a strong source of security that our actions are influenced. When that happens we are taking actions that are governed by associations with material things instead of by associations with the laws of God. Then, there is no hope for maximizing security.

If you desire strongly something that someone else possesses, you are only hurting yourself. This is a danger from association chains. The problem is that you associate someone else's source of security as your source of security. (This is not the same as love where the security level of the other person can affect your security level.) You are associating security with what the other person possesses. Since you associate security with something that you can not possess, this desire becomes a source of frustration and, therefore, causes insecurity. If any action is taken toward obtaining your neighbor's possessions, the laws of "do not steal" and "do not kill" assert themselves. Since no action can obtain the security of the other person's possessions, the coveter tends to take no action. This means he takes no actions to increase his own level of security. He does not solve his own problems and end his insecurity. His level of security decreases. To desire your neighbor's spouse or his house does you no good whatsoever.

Besides, that particular spouse or that particular house may not even give you the security that it gives him. Things that you associate with security and enjoy are not exactly like his associations of security. He may like a big fireplace. You may like a small one.

This does not mean that you should not want things like other people have. Building a house like your neighbor's because you like his house is all right. You are working to maximize your security.

There can be associations that are so strong that they overpower our search to maximize our security. You must be aware of these associations and work against them. Jesus said, "Let the dead bury their dead ...". (Luke9:60) The dead are gone. They will not return. Their departure is a loss of security for us. We can associate the loss others feel with the way we would feel if someone that close to us died. However, Christianity has only two time periods; the present and the future.

There are things to do. Mourning the dead will not help them and will only give you associations that will make you feel insecure. While you mourn the dead, you are not solving your real problems and this will cause you insecurity. Furthermore, you are missing opportunities to gain security.

You are not required to seek to maximize your security by following the same sources of security that everyone else does. Of course, on the other hand, you may if that will maximize your security. It is not difficult to understand that some people could be born with physical or mental reasons that make them incapable of marriage. There are others who have had their associations hurt so badly by their fellow man that they are incapable of marriage because they can not associate security with another person.

It is not clear what Jesus meant by renouncing marriage "for the sake of the kingdom of Heaven." It could be interpreted to mean that strong

Christians should not get married. It certainly is an endorsement of celibacy. In many cultures the unmarried person is looked down upon and ridiculed. Jesus is against this. Two things are certain. Jesus recommends marriage for those who can handle it and He sees nothing wrong with not getting married.

Maximizing security means evaluating your associations and restraints. It means altering associations and taking the time to examine your association chains. It means taking the time to think about what you are doing. All this requires a low priority environment and time. And, it should be done on a regular basis. Rest and relaxation, peace and quiet are extremely valuable to us. It is unfortunate that we forget or do not realize this. Once a week, take off for 24 consecutive hours and relax.

Work to develop the associations you are supposed to have. "Be pure in heart." It is difficult to act based on an association that is half-hearted, not strong. Being pure in heart means having developed the proper associations and having avoided the improper ones. That is a difficult task, but something to work toward.

We always say that people can not be perfect and that is probably true, but Jesus is telling us to try. To be perfect means to follow the teachings of Jesus.

There is a lot said in the world now about self-esteem. The idea is that we should all try to be whatever we want to be. Many people are not doing this, it is said, because they have low self-esteem. My guess is that their security level is so low that they are just trying to build enough determination to get through the day.

Nonetheless, if your self-esteem is helped by the praise of others and hurt by the criticism of others, you have the wrong associations. It does not matter what others think of you. It only matters what God thinks of you. Are you following His laws? If you are, you are getting the maximum security and developing the maximum security level for the environment you find yourself in. If you are, then you should know that you are in control and that should mean that self-esteem is not a problem for you.

It seems to me that one of the more basic teachings of the modern Christian church is that sin is fun, but it is bad. Eventually, a person feels guilty eating a piece of candy.

Sin is anything that does not allow a person to maximize his security. It does not have to be an action; it can be an association. Adultery is looking with a lustful eye, as well as a sexual action. Sin is a thought or action that is contrary to the laws of God.

Sin is not determined by the thoughts of society. If your neighbors consider an action of yours to be sinful, that does not make it a sin. A sin is not something the individual associates with security or insecurity. If we help a dirty old man who has fallen by the road, that is not a sin. However, our neighbors may frown on us for being with such a person and we may feel very insecure for being with such a dirty, distasteful person. However, the sin would be in not helping the old man. This, of course, is the point Jesus makes when He tells the famous parable of the Good Samaritan.

It has always bothered me that sinning is considered to be fun. Nevertheless, it is generally true because there is security to be gained from sin. The point is, of course, that the security from sin is not the maximum security that you could have. If a man goes into town and gets drunk on Saturday night, he feels secure and this increases his security. Remember that associations and feelings exist in only one point in time. They have nothing to do with what will happen in the future. After all, people who get drunk usually wake up the next day feeling miserable. Such is the security from sinning.

Since sin may give security, there must be an idea that the security gained from sin could be used to form restraints that would prevent you from sinning again. There are two things wrong with that idea. First, you should maximize your security and that can not be done by sinning. Second, sinful security makes the sin a source of security. This creates an association of security with that sin. This association needs to be overcome to form a restraint against that sin.

There is an idea in our culture that sinners are better off than non-sinners. Crimes are committed and the criminals are never caught. (But, criminals do get caught.)

The real punishment to the sinner is not the actions taken against him by others. His real punishment is the associations he possesses that have lead him to sin as a source of security. The whole life of the insensitive decreaser-of-the-security-of-others is such that he would have to make major changes in his associations and actions to have any hope of maximizing his security. In his environment he will never have the same level of security as a follower of the laws of God.

Unfortunately, we are all only human and that means that at some time we will sin. A person must be careful of what he does after the sin has been committed. If he shrugs it off and forgets that it happened; he will be just as likely to commit that sin again.

If you sin, be aware that you have sinned and form an association of insecurity toward the sin. Be aware of the circumstances that broke down your restraints or associations and thus allowed the sin to occur. Prevent that set of circumstances from occurring again. If necessary, build associations and restraints that you may not have had.

Do not feel great guilt and associations of insecurity because you have sinned. This only reduces your level of security and makes you more likely to sin again. Jesus taught that if you ask forgiveness of your sins; God will forgive you. By asking for forgiveness you are acknowledging to yourself that you have sinned and you have acknowledged that this is bad and you should not do it again. God's forgiveness allows you to start over NOW, no matter how much you have sinned. It means that you need not feel guilty (thus feeling insecure and lowering your security level) and you have no reason to continue sinning. The situation is not hopeless; you can stop now.

RULES TO EVALUATE OTHERS

Because they can affect your security, it is sometimes necessary to evaluate the ideas and actions of others. (This is not judging others; that is something else.) The following laws relate to this:

HONOR THY FATHER AND THY MOTHER. (Exod.20:12)
KNOW FALSE PROPHETS BY THE RESULTS OF THEIR ACTIONS.

Jesus said, "Beware of false prophets, men who come to you dressed up as sheep while underneath they are savage wolves. You will recognize them by the fruits they bear." (Matt.7:15-16)

Honoring your parents does not necessarily mean obeying them. If we obeyed them absolutely, we would learn and accept their culture and not change it. Mankind would cease to advance and we would be worshipping society instead of God. This commandment means our parents should be listened to and taken care of. They should not be insulted or humiliated. If you disagree with your parents, you should consider what they have to say. Do not argue at length with them about it. Make your decision and go your way.

There is a reason for honoring your parents. If you do not, you will create an association of insecurity toward them. This association will also be linked to what your parents have tried to teach you. It will hurt the restraints they have tried to build in you. Remember that our parents represent a culture that has acquired knowledge of what gives security. It is based on the associations of many generations. This culture is not perfect, but parts of it are correct. Included in this culture are the rules of God that have become part of your culture and are taught to you as "the right thing to do". The culture of your parents contains knowledge that should not be turned away lightly.

Beware of accepting an idea because it sounds good. Someone may have just lead you down an association chain. This can cause you to associate security with an action that some of your other associations would not have associated with security. Consider the consequences ("fruits") of actions or ideas. If they do not maximize your security, you have been lead down an inaccurate association chain by a "false prophet".

RULES TO DEVELOP PROPER ASSOCIATIONS TOWARD OTHERS

Before interacting with others, there are some associations you should have that control your attitude toward them. Regardless of your situation, these are the associations you want to have. The following laws relate to this:

DO NOT JUDGE OTHERS. Jesus said, "Pass no judgement, and you will not be judged. For as you judge others, so will yourselves be judged, and whatever you deal out to others will be dealt back to you." (Matt.7:1-2)
BE HUMBLE. Jesus said, "How blest are those who know that they are poor; the kingdom of heaven is theirs." (Matt.5:3) Jesus said, "Let a man humble himself till he is like this child, and he will be the greatest in the kingdom of Heaven."(Matt.18:4)
MOURN. Jesus said, "How blest are the sorrowful; they shall find consolation." (Matt.5:4)
LOVE YOUR ENEMY. (Matt.5:44-45)
BLESS THEM THAT CURSE YOU. (Luke6:28)

Judging others has to be my favorite sin because almost everyone does it. They do not know it is a sin, and it is much more damaging to the person doing it than it is to the victim.

There is a difference between evaluating someone and judging them. An evaluation examines the actions of another to see how they affect your security. A judgement is applying your associations to another person (their looks, actions, etc.). There is no relationship between your associations and the associations someone else has, nor should there be. Judgements are calling people names, deciding by looking at them what kind of people they are and how they will act, or deciding what kind of person someone is from your associations toward the group to which you think they belong.

Judging means assuming what people will do next, how they will act and think. If you believe you know how someone will act, you will not communicate with them because you think you know what they are thinking. Since you will not communicate, they will not know how to communicate with you or how to give you security. You will miss their knowledge and friendship.

Humility, on the other hand, has many advantages. A humble person will tend to be associated with security by his fellow men. He will not act in a manner to appear better than others. Jesus tells us that when we are asked to an important event, we should sit at a humble place, not at the most honored place. This way we may be asked to come forward, but we will not be asked to move down. (Luke14:8-11)

The most important advantage to humility is that it allows us to learn. Jesus said, "Whoever receives a prophet as a prophet will be given a prophet's reward, ...". (Matt.10:41) It is very much a mistake to assume that your own associations of security will maximize your security. You must be humble and listen to others. Other people are also seeking to maximize their own security. They have acquired associations from environments that you have not experienced. This knowledge can be valuable if interpreted correctly. Some of it can be accepted; some of it must be discarded. If you do not feel that you are "poor", you will have too strong an association of security with your own associations and you will not learn as easily.

People who are sorrowful (those who mourn) are sensitive to other people. Such persons will try to avoid decreasing the security of others and will receive security from their sensitivity with others.

As to loving your enemies and blessing those who curse you, there is no reason for you to have an association of insecurity toward someone just because they have such an association toward you. If you love your enemies, you will have no trouble working with them. You will not have an association of insecurity prevent you from making a decision that will benefit both parties. Politicians often have to work with their political enemies. Political "enemies" means there is a disagreement most of the time, but not always. Two "enemies" will agree on the same thing and will work hard together to see their law passed. At the same time they will work against each other over a different law. Without this loving of enemies, democratic governments would have a hard time working.

You gain no security from hate. It only creates associations in you that will prevent you from seeking to maximize your security. Hate leads you to take actions that make the other person insecure; not actions that maximize your security. After World War One the German people were persecuted and bitterness and economic depression were the result. This was to blame, at least in part, for World War Two. Hate hurt everyone involved. After World War Two, the German people received a more just peace and economic assistance. This gave the United States a strong friend and helped the economy of everyone.

If you increase your enemy's security, how long can he remain your enemy? Indeed, you become one of his sources of security and he begins to associate you with security (which must really confuse him.) Loving your enemy allows you to follow God's other rules, without having to overcome an association within yourself.

Strengthen yourself by developing strong associations with God, so that these associations can not be compromised by associations with your other sources of security. Strengthen yourself also by developing strong associations toward others, such as respecting your parents, loving your enemies, not judging others, being sensitive, and being humble. All this will be to your benefit when you come into conflict with your fellow human beings.

Chapter Nine

RULES OF GOD RELATING TO OTHERS

The essence of man's relationship with his fellow man is the ability to manipulate or eliminate his fellow man. Jesus is mainly concerned with this problem. When a person seeks to maximize his security, he is sometimes going to get in the way of someone else seeking his security. This is conflict.

There are three areas of conflict to be discussed in this chapter. First is violent conflict. This is the situation of physical attack - how to avoid it and what to do about it. Second is conflict with a group - the individual against society. Third is conflict of a nonviolent nature between individuals - how to handle arguments and influence people.

VIOLENCE

The nonviolent nature of Christian teaching is well known. The major part of this idea is to give in to force so completely as to increase its security. Then to retreat as far as possible from it, and not create associations of insecurity toward yourself. The following laws relate to this:

TURN THE OTHER CHEEK. Jesus said, "You have learned that they were told, 'An eye for an eye, and a tooth for a tooth.' But what I tell you is this: Do not set yourself against the man who wrongs you. If someone slaps you on the right cheek, turn and offer him your left." (Matt.5:38-39)

BE WISE AS SERPENTS, HARMLESS AS DOVES. Jesus said, "Behold, I send you forth as sheep in the midst of wolves: be ye therefore wise as serpents, and harmless as doves." (Matt.10:16)

WHEN YOU ARE PERSECUTED IN ONE TOWN, MOVE ON. (Matt.10:23)

SUFFER PERSECUTION. Jesus said, "How blest are those who have suffered persecution for the cause of right; the kingdom of heaven is theirs. How blest you are, when you suffer insults and persecution and every kind of calumny for my sake." (Matt.5:10-12)

DO NOT KILL. (Exod.20:13)

BEWARE OF MEN. Jesus said, "... beware of men: for they will deliver you up to the councils, ...". (Matt.10:17)

If you are made insecure by someone, you must not respond with an action that attempts to make them insecure. You are not maximizing your security, you are only lowering someone else's. This causes no good to yourself and creates an association of insecurity toward you in the other person. This will probably result in more insecurity being done to you by him. While the two of you are lowering each other's security, you are not using your time to acquire security—you both lose.

Jesus tells Peter (Matt.17:24-27) to pay a tax even though they, as citizens, should be exempt, because there is some confusion over their status. He gives in to a powerful foe, even though that opponent is wrong, to avoid jail or worse. Jesus says nothing of honor or pride. He only says to avoid trouble by any means and to do others no harm. Jesus says that God will give you the words to speak when arrested and persecuted and asked to speak (Matt.10:17-20). Later, when Jesus has been arrested and Peter questioned about Him, Peter denies knowledge of Jesus. Only the teachings of Jesus are truth, not the code of honor or the principles of society.

Death is the ultimate insecurity. To have caused it in another person, causes you to be associated with insecurity by everyone, including yourself. Your action will cause the victim's friends to associate you with insecurity. To kill is to invite great revenge as well as to deprive the world of the greatest resource God gave it—the individual human being.

Throughout man's existence, killing has always been a short term solution to any conflict between people. This solution is to be avoided. It prevents compromise and an exchange of ideas.

Jesus does make one reference to violence. He said, "You must not think that I have come to bring peace to the earth; I have not come to bring peace, but a sword. I have come to set a man against his father, a daughter against her mother, a young wife against her mother-in-law; and a man will find his enemies under his own roof." (Matt.10:34-36)

Here are two ideas that seem to conflict. One is "turn the other cheek" and the other is "I have come to bring a sword". It has to be difficult to resolve the two so that they do not contradict one another.

What do you do if you see someone about to be killed? If you could do something and did not, you could consider yourself to be an accessory to murder. That would mean you were going to break the "shall not kill" commandment anyway. Jesus never says anything specifically about this situation. If He had, it might have been misinterpreted. The only vague reference we have is the sword quote. This is very vague, but it is an admission of violence.

Natural laws lead to a series of associations creating restraints and courses of action that will cause us to do the Christian thing in any circumstances. The greater the priority level of the environment, the less affect associations and restraints have on our action. If you are about to be run over by a car, you get out of the way regardless of any restraint against running on the sidewalk. We can well assume that the associations of the natural laws break down when it comes to a matter of self-defense.

There is a need for a logical explanation as to when the sword should be used. That explanation is to use what God put within us—seek your own security. If you can run to avoid killing, then run. If you are only going to get yourself killed, then do not fight. The important point is that you must not hurt your aggressor any more than is necessary to stop him. Once he is stopped, it is the duty of the Christian to instill in his enemy an association of security toward him. "Is your security threatened?" and, "How much is it threatened?" have got to be the basis for the Christian response.

You are unlikely to face situations that involve either self-defense or overwhelming opposition. The use of violence should be there for your own security. However, its use is for crisis only. It does not win the conflict—it only prevents your loss. The opposition must cease to be the opposition and the only way to do that is to make them associate you with security. If you kill your enemy, then you have the loss of security to yourself as related when discussing "thou shalt not kill."

Violence is a permissible tool, but a good Christian should make every effort to avoid it since it does not give him any real increase in security.

GROUP CONFLICT

Conflict with a group, especially our own group, is difficult. First, there is the influence of the group upon us as an individual that must not be allowed to affect our associations with God. Second, there is our need to influence the group. Third, there is the responsibility placed on the group, and on us as an individual member, for the actions of the group.

A group is a society. It has a powerful influence on its members because it gives security to those who follow its course of action. It gives insecurity to those who go against its rules. To those who follow, there is the companionship and security from its members. For those who do not, there is the threat of being ignored. For those who depend on a group as a major source of security, this threat is almost impossible to resist.

Society, the group, tends to conflict with the laws of God. There was a previous discussion of the laws whose purpose is to resist attempts to alter your associations with God. These laws are: have no other gods, have no idols, do not take the name of God in vain, give alms to God in secret, fast in private, and pray in private.

Generally speaking, God does not like society. Its power is too strong and it is not following God in all its rules. It is too much like a god itself. Although society tends to adopt rules that increase or even maximize the individual's security, more often they merely increase one's security in a limited time period. When you break society's rules, you are punished. When God's law is contrary to the society's, you must make a decision. Those who remain strongly in the society, do so because they follow the society's rules. They justify compromises and different interpretations of the laws of God. For this reason, Jesus complains, "You have made God's law null and void out of respect for your tradition." (Matt.15:6)

Jesus does not want you to create a link between your associations toward religion and your associations toward society. If man does this, the society will begin to control the religion and the man. Jesus said, "Be careful not to make a show of your religion before men; if you do, no reward awaits you in your Father's house in heaven. ... Thus, when you do some act of charity, do not announce it with a flourish of trumpets ... your good deed must be secret, ... Again, when you pray, do not be like the hypocrites; they love to say their prayers standing up in synagogue and at the street corners, for everyone to see them. I tell you this: they have their reward already. But when you pray, go into a room by yourself, shut the door, and pray ...". (Matt.6:1-6) It is sinful to pray in public and there is a very good reason why this is so. Actions that are intended to maximize your security over time require an association of security with the action and its result. If you pray in public or do good in public, your security comes from society. It is their praise and friendship that is your reward. If they approve of the action, you have received the security to continue that action. It is the standards of your culture that you are following.

The Christian will find himself acting contrary to the rules of society. Its members will form associations of insecurity against him, but the security he gives to the society will offset some of this.

Jesus is not in favor of doing away with society. He said, "For where two or three have met together in my name, "I am there among them." (Matt.18:20) People working together can help each other to find the correct way and work to carry it out. However, the kind of society that Jesus must want should not have laws contrary to those of God. This means that each person must be allowed to seek to maximize his own security. It means that each individual must do what he thinks God wants him to do, not what his friends want him to do.

After resisting society's attempt to influence you away from the laws of God, it is your turn. Your duty, as a Christian, is to teach others. The following laws relate to this:

TEACH. Jesus said, "What I say to you in the dark you must repeat in broad daylight; ...". (Matt.10:27)

GO AND TEACH ALL NATIONS, BAPTIZING THEM. (Matt.28:19-20)

IF YOUR BROTHER SINS, TALK, GO TO CHURCH, IGNORE HIM. Jesus said, "If your brother commits a sin, go and take the matter up with him, strictly between yourselves, and if he listens to you, you have won your brother over. If he will not listen, take one or two others with you, so that all facts may be duly established on the evidence of two or three witnesses. If he refuses to listen to them, report the matter to the congregation; and if he will not listen even to the congregation, you must then treat him as you would a pagan or a tax-gatherer." (Matt.18:15-17)

ALLOW CHILDREN TO LEARN OF GOD. Jesus said, "Suffer little children, and forbid them not, to come unto me: for of such is the kingdom of heaven." (Matt.19:14)

DO NOT BE CALLED MASTER. Jesus said, "Neither be ye called masters: for one is your master, ...". (Matt.23:10)

LET YOUR LIGHT SHINE. Jesus said, "And you, like the lamp, must shed light among your fellows, so that, when they see the good you do, they may give praise to your Father in heaven." (Matt.5:16)

Influencing others by teaching them the things Jesus teaches is the duty of every Christian, but if you tell other people they are sinning, you will create insecure associations toward you and your ideas. The question is really one of how much you should try to influence your fellow man and how you should go about doing it.

The law "if your brother sins, talk, go to church, ignore him" is pretty aggressive action. Note that Jesus uses "brother" and not "neighbor". We can assume then that he is suggesting this course of action for someone who is close to you. The reason for this is that their association of security toward you should be greater that the association of insecurity caused by your criticism of them. Hopefully, the security associated with you (or the witnesses and congregation) and with the logic of your argument and the evidence will be great enough to overcome the security associated with the sinful course of action. If he continues to sin, ignoring him will keep him from influencing others and perhaps will persuade him to give up the sin. The loss of security may create associations of insecurity in him toward his actions. It will certainly create associations of insecurity toward his actions in other members of the group. In addition, it will prevent you from being drawn into the insecurities his sins will cause. The use of witnesses and evidence suggests that Jesus requires a solid evaluation for this type of procedure, not just a judgement.

Notice that Jesus wants you to make every effort possible to reach the other person and show them how to maximize their security. He also wants you to have witnesses of your complaint. This will ensure that you are warning him of a real sin and that when he is ignored, the other members of the society will know why this action was taken. Being part of this will make the group associate the action with security and the sin with insecurity.

Influencing someone who is not your brother is a different problem. Ignoring someone who does not know you exist is hardly an effective weapon of influence. Teaching is.

Not everyone will have the proper associations to accept the teachings of Jesus. Jesus said, "Do not give dogs what is holy; do not feed your pearls to pigs: they will only trample on them, and turn and tear you to pieces." (Matt.7:6) Learning a fact or idea requires a proper association or association chain. Some people do not have the suitable associations or they have contrary associations that are just too strong. When faced with this situation, the teacher should leave. If he does not, he may be associated with insecurity by the pupil. After all, if the student can not learn, it is because the teacher is going contrary to some association of security. This will cause an association of insecurity to be formed against the teacher. If the Christian's ideas are not accepted, then he should not force them, but should go somewhere else where he will be heard.

Influence those who are not prepared to be taught by showing and telling them the results of Christianity. This is one purpose of the "Let your light shine" law. After all, everyone is seeking what they perceive to be their own individual security. All you have to do is show them the security and how to get it.

Include children when Christianity is taught. Children should learn the correct restraints and associations as soon as possible. If they have to change from incorrect restraints and associations, they should do so sooner when it is easier.

Be sure of what you are teaching. Our society needs rules. We need laws for our governments. We need rules for our work place. We need rules for our culture. We need people to make these rules and we need people to enforce them. It is easy and convenient to consider our rules to be perfect, but they are not. We must not allow ourselves to develop a stronger association with our own rules than with God's. We must not be called "master", only God is "master".

Jesus makes sure that we still realize that we are our brother's keeper. "If the master has been called Beelzebub, how much more his household!" (Matt.10:25) Those who are in a group causing insecurity to others are victims of that insecurity in the same way that individuals are of the insecurity they cause. The problem is which action the innocent member of a bad group should take. If the group is too powerful, you must leave the direct vicinity of that group and live away from them. At other times you can work within the group. The idea of group responsibility should lead you to two lessons; responsibility to your fellow man and the realization that you are part of your group and should leave it if it becomes uncontrollable and a causer of insecurity.

INDIVIDUAL CONFLICT

Personal conflict—nonviolent, everyday interaction with our fellow man, is our most common conflict. This is what we do each time we meet someone. And, doing this right is not easy. It is necessary to be nice to others, to not cause harm to others, to deal properly with sex issues, and to be a positive influence.

If you are nice to other people, if you give them security, they will associate you with security which is always to your advantage. The following laws relate to this:

LOVE YOUR NEIGHBOR. (Matt.22:39)

GIVE WHEN ASKED. Jesus said, "Give to every man that asketh of thee; and of him that taketh away thy goods ask them not again." (Luke6:30)

IF SUED, SETTLE QUICKLY. Jesus said, "If someone sues you, come to terms with him promptly while you are both on your way to court; otherwise he may hand you over to the judge, ... and you will be put in jail." (Matt.5:25)

BE MEEK. Jesus said, "How blest are those of gentle spirit; they shall have the earth for their possession." (Matt.5:5)

BE MERCIFUL. Jesus said, "How blest are those who show mercy; mercy shall be shown them." (Matt.5:7)

FORGIVE. Jesus said, "For if you forgive others the wrongs they have done, your heavenly Father will also forgive you; but if you do not forgive others, then the wrongs you have done will not be forgiven by your Father." (Matt.6:14-15)

TREAT OTHERS AS YOU WOULD HAVE THEM TREAT YOU. Jesus said, "Always treat others as you would like them to treat you: that is the Law and the prophets." (Matt.7:12)

Treat your neighbors well and associate them with security. If you consider the consequences of your actions on the security of your neighbor, you should be able to give him security, not insecurity. If you associate your neighbor with security, you should be able to deal with him in a friendly and equitable manner. This should prevent conflicts or, at least, settle them quickly and easily.

Conflicts must be settled in an equitable manner, if at all possible. Jesus said that if someone sues you for your coat, then give him your shirt also. As a Christian, it may be easy to manipulate others so that you always have them at your advantage. However, if you do not make an equitable settlement, then you have not settled the conflict. At the moment of settlement, both people may have feelings of security that are the result of association chains. These chains will break down in a short period of time. If the settlement has not brought enough security to overcome the insecurity of the conflict, then there will be more insecurity and conflict. This is true for both parties. Do not make a settlement that is unfair to the other person. It will only cause him to associate you with insecurity. On the other hand, you should not cheat yourself either. Otherwise, you will associate the other person with insecurity and the conflict will continue. Make an equitable settlement of your conflicts. When there is some dispute in your mind about how well you did, settle anyway and remember Jesus' comment about giving the other person your shirt.

Jesus said that the meek shall inherit the earth. It is important to remember that you can be ambitious and aggressive and still be meek. Aggression and ambition describe the goal of a person's actions. "Gentle spirit" is how you are perceived by others. Meekness is how you should be viewed by your fellow man as you try to maximize your security. If you are not meek, you will create associations of insecurity in other people toward yourself. At best, this will cause them to avoid you. People who receive the support of others are those who have an association of security toward them by others. These are the people of "gentle spirit". Meekness does not mean that you never take a strong stand or say "no". It only means that you do so with tact and a smile.

Jesus also said, "Be ye therefore merciful, as your Father also is merciful." (Luke6:36) To show mercy is to increase someone else's security at a time when they are feeling insecure. This creates a strong association of security in the other person toward the one who showed mercy. It also creates a strong association of security toward the act of showing mercy, in the person who benefited.

Mercy also means acting without punishment. Cutting off the hand of a thief is a punishment. It makes the person from whom he stole feel better. It does nothing to maximize anyone's security. Mercy does not mean failure to act. Something must be done to prevent the thief from stealing in the future, but what is done should be done to maximize everyone's security. (Put him in prison where he can not steal and try to rehabilitate him.)

Failure to forgive others affects your ability to get along with the other person. This means that for the insecurity you suffered, you will take action that will result in denying yourself future security from that person. You have therefore done more insecurity to yourself than the other person ever did to you. If a friend insults you or embarrasses you and you never have anything to do with them again, you have lost more by your decision than by anything they ever did.

If we fail to forgive, then we are thinking or seeking revenge. This will not maximize our security. It is a difficult idea to grasp. When someone causes us insecurity, we associate them with insecurity. We naturally try to get rid of this insecurity and the most immediate way is to purge it. This is done by countering the insecure association with a secure association which is likely to be one of dominance over the cause of insecurity. First of all, revenge keeps the association of insecurity on a high conscious level and this causes insecurity because it makes us feel insecure. Secondly, we are not trying to maximize our own security, only decrease that of someone else.

If you do not forgive, the other person will know that you have an association of insecurity against him. He will then avoid you (if he is acting in a Christian manner). He may decide to get you before you get him. He could cause you much insecurity.

If you forgive others, you are combating an association of insecurity. Any association has the power to affect your security level because you think about it and that gives you the feeling associated with the association. If you lessen the strength of an insecure association (by forgiving), it will decrease your security less when you think about it.

Forgiving is an act of kindness. This increases the security of someone who has decreased your security. This will decrease their association of insecurity against you and will make you a source of security for them.

There are more subtle reasons to forgive. If you forgive the other person, you counter any associations of insecurity that you may have against them. It may be difficult to completely counter them, but you must work at it.

Forgiveness, like being humble, gives flexibility of action. If you counter the insecure association, then you can give and receive security from the person forgiven. It also allows you to evaluate the other person with a minimum of association interference. The other person can then be approached without showing insecurity against that person. This means they can give you advice and help and they are much more easily manipulated. Often in the legislature, two people will oppose each other about whether a bill should become law. If they become bitter and revengeful over the dispute, they will not be able to work well together. This is not acceptable to them because the next bill may be one they agree on. It is to their advantage to forget past disputes and work together to manipulate others to vote for their bill.

After Jesus was killed, the early Christians could have formed terrorist units and attacked the Romans and the Jewish leadership. This would have been revenge and they did not do it. Later, the Jews attacked the Romans with disastrous results. The Christians conquered the Roman Empire three hundred years after the death of Jesus. They did not do it with acts of violence and revenge. They did it with humility and forgiveness—they subverted it from within. They used other people's associations of security. The person who is humble and forgives has great flexibility in his course of action. He creates in others, associations of security toward himself. These two things make it easier for him to manipulate others in personal conflict.

As to "Give when asked", you should not have such a strong association of security toward your material goods that it should cause you such insecurity in giving them up. Of course, if your security is going to be badly damaged because you give when asked, then don't give that much. If someone comes to the door and asks you to give him your home, give him a little money and send him on his way. If you find that you have little to give when asked, perhaps you should examine the way you are spending your money. I do not think Jesus would approve of our being so much in debt just to have a better lifestyle. Perhaps we should have smaller, more affordable houses and more money in our pocket.

Jesus said, "Always treat others as you would like them to treat you: that is the Law and the prophets." (Matt.7:12) You should give security to your fellow man, not insecurity. If you give security, your fellow man will tend to associate you with security. This means you will receive security (or less insecurity) from him.

It is just not to your advantage to cause insecurity in others. The following laws relate to this:

DO NOT STEAL. (Exod.20:15)
DO NOT BEAR FALSE WITNESS AGAINST YOUR NEIGHBOR. (Exod.20:16)

When you steal, you decrease someone else's security. If you are discovered or suspected, it creates an association of insecurity toward you in other people. This is never to your advantage. It can result in other people causing you insecurity; such as sending you to prison or refusing you the security of their society.

The most basic reason not to steal is based on an association of sensitivity to others. If you have that association, then stealing will give you associations of insecurity because you will feel you have caused someone else insecurity. If you do not have that association, you have already lost a great many opportunities for security.

One of the ten commandments is "Thou shalt not bear false witness against thy neighbor." (Exod.20:16) Everyone seems to be under the impression that it is sinful to lie. That is not what this commandment says. It is obvious that you are not supposed to lie under oath to cause insecurity to a neighbor. Such a lie will cause an association of insecurity toward yourself. This can cause things to happen that will cause you insecurity. After all, perjury (lying under oath) is a crime.

Of all our relationships with other individuals, the sexual relationship is probably the most critical to our security. The following laws relate to this:

DO NOT COMMIT ADULTERY. (Exod.20:14)
ADULTERY IS LOOKING WITH LUST. Jesus said, "whosoever looketh on a woman to lust after her hath committed adultery with her already in his heart." (Matt.5:28)
ADULTERY IS MARRYING A WOMAN DIVORCED, NOT FOR ADULTERY. Jesus said, "If a man divorces his wife for any case other than unchastity he involves her in adultery; and anyone who marries a woman so divorced commits adultery." (Matt.5:32)
ADULTERY IS DIVORCE AND REMARRY. Jesus said, "Whoever divorces his wife and marries another commits adultery against her: so to, if she divorces her husband and marries another, she commits adultery." (Mark10:11-12)
DO NOT DISRUPT A MARRIAGE. In speaking of marriage, Jesus said, "What God has joined together, man must not separate." (Matt.19:6)

In a love relationship, each person is a strong source of security for the other. Each associates their own security with the other's security. Each is happier and more secure if the other is happy and each feels insecure if the other feels insecure. This is the association that binds the marriage together. Sex must be a source of security for each spouse and that source of security must be associated with the spouse, and only the spouse.

Adultery is not just having sex with someone to whom you are not married. It is the creation of an association that is contrary to the association of love and security toward one's spouse. This can be done by an action or just a thought that creates the offending association. Sex with someone else is the act that can attack the marriage association. Lust is the thought that can attack the marriage association.

Lust is a sin. It is thoughts (associations) of a sexually explicit nature that do not consider the security of the partner.

There is no mention here of marriage. Marriage is not permission to lust after your partner. Lust is sex or sexually explicit thoughts that do not consider the security and happiness of your spouse (or yourself). This means that if you lust after the person to whom you are married, it is adultery, a sin, and it will weaken your marriage.

Noticing that someone is attractive is not sexually explicit enough to be lust. Being attractive is not a sin. (You are not responsible for the thoughts of others.) Being attractive to your spouse (dressing up or down) is not a sin as long as it is done with associations of security for both you and your spouse.

Avoiding lust means that sex must always be for the enjoyment of both partners. After all, if a sexual act gives insecurity or creates an association of insecurity in the other partner, it is destroying the marriage association and is, therefore, adultery.

Jesus is fairly explicit in saying that you could divorce for adultery, can not remarry if you are divorced, and can not marry a person who is divorced.

Does this mean you can never remarry? Can you remarry if your spouse commits adultery and leaves? Can you remarry if your spouse does terrible things to you or your children and you leave? Can you remarry if you have grown apart and are totally incompatible and miserable and you have met a nice person? If it is permissible to kill someone if they are about to kill someone else, why is it not permissible to remarry under certain circumstances?

Jesus does not say anything against leaving a marriage. So, if you are unhappy, you can do that. Divorce and remarry, however, are serious subjects.

There is a temptation toward adultery because we tend to associate a lot of security with sex. When things go wrong in our lives, there is a temptation to turn to sex for security.

If you are not getting along with your partner, it may be that you are not giving enough security. Work it out; changing partners is not the answer. You must learn to live with someone. The solution is not to find another sexual partner.

Why does Jesus give permission to divorce if adultery has been committed? Adultery can dissolve the marriage if one partner no longer has any association of security with the other.

Adultery does not mandate divorce. It shows a serious problem which you can deal with as you like.

Divorce does not give you permission to remarry and you do not have permission to marry someone who is divorced.

Marriage requires the development of the marriage association (each associates security with the other's security) before the marriage takes place. If that association has been created before and then broken, it will be harder to recreate that association again. A lot of insecurity has been attached to that association as the marriage unraveled and fell apart. Overcoming that insecurity and building a strong, secure association will be difficult. Furthermore, the creation of insecurities that destroyed the marriage must be prevented from occurring again. Do you know what you did to help create those insecurities and have you corrected your actions and associations? The breakup of the marriage caused a lot of insecurity and, if you go through it again, it will again cause you a lot of insecurity.

A person marrying someone who has been divorced is committing adultery because he is having a sexual relationship that may not be based on a marriage association, but on sexual desire alone. The association of security he has with the person he is marrying can not be too strong because that person's associations with him are not too strong. Consequently, the relationship will not result in the maximum security that a marriage relationship can give.

We probably can divorce and remarry, but only under the same sort of extreme circumstances that may give us permission to kill. You may consider it a question of your own security. Assume that Jesus wants us to maximize our own security over time. If divorce and/or remarry will do that for you, then it is permissible. However, do not take that lightly! Maximizing security does not mean marrying the best looking or richest person you can find. If your marriage failed, there was a reason and you may be half of it. You need to discover what there was within you that was the cause and you need to repair those associations. If you can make those repairs while you are still married and save the marriage, you are much better off. If the marriage is over, be very cautious about marrying again! You did something wrong the first time, even if it was in choice of partner. If you have not learned anything, you should not remarry. If the previous marriage is over because one partner no longer has associations of security with the other and you have created an association of security with the new partner's security (the marriage association) and, if you have found your errors and corrected them, you may remarry.

Is lust the great hidden negative security of our existence? Is this the thing that destroys our relationships? Sex is so much fun and has so much security associated with it. It has all these secondary associations attached to it: trust, caring, support for the future, security. Sex just for the sake of physical exercise creates an association of insecurity in your partner. (They think they are being used.) This begins to destroy those other associations with sex. If sex is the great cement that holds the relationship together, creating an association of insecurity with sex will surely destroy the relationship.

Sex with love is a great source of security. It is not just for the wealthy or the lucky. It is available to every man and every woman. This means that a vast majority of people associate security with love and marriage and this association is a source of security. Any threat to love and marriage creates a large association of insecurity toward the threat. This association can show itself as violence or milder forms of action. Whatever the case, there will be no security gained by any attempt to break up a marriage.

Be a positive influence to the world around you. It will cause that world to associate you with security and it will increase the security level of that surrounding world. This has to give you more security. It's a nice circle. The following laws relate to this:

BE RECONCILED WITH YOUR BROTHER. Jesus said, "... that whosoever is angry with his brother without cause shall be in danger of the judgement: ... Therefore if thou bring thy gift to the altar, and there rememberest that thy brother hath ought against thee; Leave there thy gift before the altar, and go thy way; first be reconciled to thy brother, and then come and offer thy gift." (Matt.5:22-24)

BE A PEACEMAKER. (Matt.5:9)

WANT THAT WHICH IS RIGHT TO PREVAIL. Jesus said, "How blest are those who hunger and thirst to see right prevail, they shall be satisfied." (Matt.5:6)

There are at least two things to be learned from the law, "Be reconciled with your brother". First, it does you no good to be angry with someone, particularly someone you love. It makes you feel insecure and that lowers your security. It gives you insecure associations toward them and gives them the same insecure associations toward you. The longer it lasts, the stronger the associations become and resolving the situation becomes more difficult. In the meantime you are losing the security you get from your brother and he is losing the security that he gets from you.

Jesus said, "You have learned ... 'Do not commit murder ...'. But what I tell you is this: Anyone who nurses anger against his brother must be brought to judgement." (Matt.5:21-22) Anger is a strong association of insecurity toward something. This association is so strong that it tends to cause itself to continue. The angry person thinks insecure thoughts that cause him to link to other insecure thoughts. There is a stronger association of insecurity than is reasonable formed toward the cause of the anger. The result is a lowering of the angry person's security and an association that is misleading because the insecurity caused is not as great as the insecurity associated with that environment.

Do not start a conflict when your security is not involved. So often we tell someone to do something because that is the way we do it. If you do not like the way your wife arranges the shelves in the kitchen, forget it! It is not related to your security if you do not use the shelves. You are engaged in a legitimate conflict only if your security is involved. Otherwise, you are creating an insecure association toward yourself in other people.

Conflict puts people on a high priority level. As a result, they are not able to think as clearly and can not seek to maximize their own security as well as they should. War will disrupt commerce, decrease the size of the work force, and do other things which hurt the economy. This hurts the standard of living which decreases the security of everyone. War between individuals, not just nations, is destructive to the individuals involved.

Such a conflict can exist only if one or both of the parties is violating God's laws. The peacemaker must educate and he must get changes agreed upon. He must make sure that the solution attempts to maximize the security of everyone involved. Being able to be a peacemaker means that both parties had an association of security toward the peacemaker. Making peace means having the strongest association toward God so that one party is not favored over another. Peace making may cause diminished associations of security with the peacemaker, but it is God that counts, not the associations others have.

For the law, "want that which is right to prevail", "right" is the environment in which everyone can seek to maximize his own security with minimum interference from others. The law does not specifically say to take action. Sometimes an action will not maximize your security; there are other things to be considered. However, when it is possible to take the action, take it. Support and approve right actions. Disapprove and do not support actions that are not right. You teach your children and you influence other people with your opinion. In these ways you can have an effect. Politically, you have resources such as time and money. If someone wants your support, your thirst for right will influence him to also thirst for right since he knows that is the requirement for your support. Those who seek to see right prevail will increase their own security and that of their fellow man.

Why is there conflict? If the Christian is always turning the other check and being humble, there should be no trouble. But, these are only aspects of the way people are perceived, not the things they do. Jesus wants Christians to be aggressive and He wants them to see right prevail. This is the cause of the conflict. It changes the Christian from being a poor, humble peasant to being a leader and a dangerous adversary. The Christian tends to become influential and powerful through his actions. When he is weak, the Christian will do what he can, in a limited capacity; but when he is strong, there is nothing to stop him from engaging in extremely aggressive actions.

Chapter Ten

PROOF

The purpose of this book is to discover the Natural Laws of Human Behavior. These laws must have a logical, scientific justification and they have to be proved just as any other law of nature has to be proved. There is a proven law that says one part oxygen and two parts hydrogen combine to form water. Just so, there is a law that says being meek will maximize your security over time and that must be proved.

The predictability part of the scientific method is a logic check on the theory. If your theory says hydrogen and oxygen will combine to produce water, then you are predicting that and you need to demonstrate it. A theory can not be a description of a one-time event.

Since the security theories describe things that affect you, the individual, experiments are difficult. Interpreting the results is more difficult. You need some means of measuring the results. The theory of relativity says that light will be bent by the sun and there are instruments and techniques to measure such things. There is, however, no means to measure a law or theory on how people should act, except by the individuals themselves. The measurement must be within the individual, since he is seeking security. Security, therefore, is the means of measurement; the accuracy of laws and theories on how the individual should act is measured by the security the individual receives. The theory that gives the most security is the most accurate. Of course, that is the theory—man should seek to maximize his own security.

A test of predictability is decision making. The decision is your prediction. If you follow God's laws in making decisions, you should be able to look back at the security you gained from that decision and see that you maximized your security. The scientific method says that if God's laws are supposed to maximize your security, then following them will maximize your security. If this is what happens, then the laws are, indeed, natural laws.

Be careful in your interpretation of the results of a decision. Make sure that you take into account the results of other decisions. Remember that you may not receive large amounts of security, only that you will maximize your security given the environment within which you exist. Remember that your interpretation may be clouded by your own associations; God has no such hindrance.

For proof, a natural law is an "invariable association" between "events or properties" about which there is "universal agreement". It is my hope that this book has shown you the "invariable association" between the rules of Jesus Christ and the maximizing of security over time by the individual human being. These rules and why they maximize security over time have been discussed in the previous chapters. The use of the individual's security over time as a measurement of the accuracy of such laws has been discussed. The "universal agreement" is not here yet, but perhaps it will come.

We need more than laws. Laws and theories are not the same. A theory is a "proposition" which explains the laws that can be deduced from it, which explains those laws by using more familiar or acceptable laws, and which predicts new laws and those laws must turn out to be true. The explanation in a theory "is always based on an analogy" with known laws. Darwin's laws of the survival of a species were used as the analogy for the first theory of security and that theory was used as the analogy for the next two theories of security. For Campbell (see chapter one), the proof of a theory is the universal acceptance of its explanation and its ability to predict new laws which gain universal acceptance. If the theory can do that, it is proven.

There is a new law from security theory. Following Jesus means each of us can maximize our own security over time. How can we do that and not interfere with each other? How can one person maximizing his security, not cause insecurity to another? Isn't it a powerful proof if the rules from Jesus can do just that?

As each individual seeks what he perceives to be security, he may occasionally come into conflict because his actions to get security will cause insecurity to others. Each individual following the laws of Jesus can not decrease the security of others because if that happened, those laws would not allow each individual to maximize his own security. This is the derived, new law of the third theory of security: The individual can not maximize his security over time by decreasing someone else's security. (For the laws of Jesus to do this, there must have been some coordination between the nature of man when he was created and the laws of Jesus.)

The key to this is our associations with others. Our ability to develop associations with the associations of others (sensitivity) allows us to develop a love relationship and allows us to develop friendships and to get pleasure from the successes and accomplishments of others. Without being sensitive to the feelings of others, we could not give them security and, so, they would not give us security. Much of our enjoyment of life depends on this ability to associate with the feelings of others.

If we are sensitive to others, decreasing their security will cause us to have associations of insecurity. Thus, our own security is reduced when we cause insecurity to someone else. Those who are not sensitive have lost so much opportunity for security that they have far to go to catch up to the average person. If you follow God's laws (do unto others as you would have them do unto you), you must be sensitive to other people. This means that your association of insecurity with acts of insecurity will cause you insecurity when you commit such acts.

Hopefully, this satisfies all but the "universal agreement" criteria to prove a theory.

If we will know what to say and do if we follow the laws of Jesus, why do we need all this theory stuff? First, the theory is a teaching device to those who believe in science and disapprove of "superstition". Second, it's the way the universe is made and knowledge is not a bad thing. ("Seek and ye shall find.") Third, we need theory to better understand Jesus' laws.

He says to us to be as wise as serpents and to have right prevail. If we understand His laws and how they work, then perhaps we can have a little more knowledge to lead us to be as wise as serpents. Jesus gives us rules that if we follow, we will make the right decisions. But, some of us don't follow as well as we should. We have other associations and we don't know if they are wrong or contrary to God, really. And, sometimes when we think we are following God, we feel uneasy and we don't know if it is our bad associations or if our bad associations have caused us to make bad decisions that our good associations are making us feel uneasy about.

Using security theory requires an evaluation of the real environment. Truth is that evaluation. Truth is two things. It is the reality of our present environment and it is the reality of future environments. Truth is the environment that is created by natural laws as a result of actions in previous environments. The environment in which you now exist is a result (at least in part) of your own actions. Truth is the future result of actions that, in part, are yours. The future environment depends on what actions are taken to solve the problems of the present environment. For instance, since man is seeking his own security and the laws of God maximize that security, then mankind is tending to move toward developing a social pattern of behavior that follows the laws of God. ("Tending" is the word. There is no guarantee we will ever develop such a society.)

The essence of using truth is to evaluate the present environment. This means being able to realize what the conditions are without associations distorting our view of reality. This means no wishful thinking that things will get better by themselves. Having recognized the situation, we can then use the rules of Jesus to maximize our security. We can do this only by taking responsibility for our own actions. Realize what has happened. Assess what you could have done differently. Do not assess what others could have done differently. Do not blame "luck". Decide what you can do in the future to avoid an insecure outcome of a situation. Act accordingly. Ignore excuses.

Since natural laws describe the real environment, violating them only ignores the inevitable. Such an act can give you enough security that you may never realize the price you paid in opportunity costs. Violations give everyone less security than they could have had. Even if one individual has such strong associations with his sources of security that he can not see his opportunity costs, others can see the losses. The bad actions and associations will receive the taint of being associated with insecurity by others.

One way to evaluate whether a law describes the real environment is to observe the consequences to an individual's security when he violates the law. Events in life are dictated by the real environment. You may avoid a large dose of insecurity or you may not. You can speed on a country road and never meet an oncoming truck, but every day you read about people who did. I suppose we could look at life as a set of probabilities, but it's really not. The person who speeds on country roads has other associations caused by the same events which caused him to speed on country roads. These cause him insecurity every day. Laws of Human Behavior determine whether his friends will go riding with him again and which friends such a person will have. Such friends will be those who associate such actions with security, probably as a purge against the insecurity caused to them by persons who would disapprove of such actions.

Natural Laws of Human Behavior must maximize our probability to survive as a species and, because the individual must survive and acts in ways that make him feel good, they must maximize the individual's quality of life over time. This is probably not the way Darwin would describe natural laws. He would say all that is required is the survival of the species. Natural laws for human beings are different. We can control our associations. Therefore, we can seek to maximize our security. God's laws benefit the individual who follows them. They must because that is the way we are made. If God's laws did not benefit the individual, we would follow other rules. Why did God make us so that our natural laws must benefit the individual? That is an irrelevant question. Maybe He just likes us. Maybe, reader, you are one of the stars in His universe.

The proof of these laws and theories must ultimately be decided by you and others to reach that ideal of "universal agreement". "Universal agreement", to be sure the theory and laws describe the real environment, requires time and study by others. Your decision will be based on your associations and, if you use these laws, on your interpretation of the results of their use.

Chapter Eleven

GROWING UP AND EDUCATION

What does all this religion and security theory mean in real life?

There is much speculation as to what is in a child's mind the moment after he is born. What instincts, what personality does he have? What have his genes given him?

The question is irrelevant! We can not control what we are born with, but we can learn and change. How much we can, does not matter. How easy it is for us, does not matter. Whatever you have is all that you have. This is your life and there is no second chance. You may be healthy or unhealthy. You may be intelligent or retarded. There is nothing you can do about it—so do what you can. Learn the things that will maximize your security in your circumstances.

Children probably learn easier than older people. Since children have not existed as long, they are either adding new associations or replacing weak ones. Furthermore, while older people have many sources of security, children have only their parents. Here then is a golden opportunity. The parents can help the child to strengthen certain associations and to build certain restraints. While the child is young, the parents can most easily teach him.

The parents need to decide what they are going to try to accomplish. It does not do much good to try to teach one thing one day and the opposite thing the next day. There are two major things to remember. First, you should teach the child those things that will maximize his security. Second, the things you associate with security are the result of your culture, they are the knowledge of the past. The child should be taught what the parent knows (the parent's culture). However, the child must not be taught the culture so strongly that he can not be different. He must be taught the rules of God so that he will have the opportunity to maximize his security. The parent's opportunity to teach the child can have great rewards for society, if the right things are taught.

The child has limitations. Associations seem to be learned easily, but they are not strong until they have been reinforced over time. Even though the child may have learned something, the association may not be strong enough to affect his actions. The result is that the child is bad, even though he "knows better".

If the child is to learn properly, the right method must be used. Obviously, the idea is fairly simple. Create associations of security with actions that maximize his security and create associations of insecurity with actions that decrease his security. It does not take an extreme action to cause either association. A word of praise, a hug, and some attention are good methods of creating security with an action. A pat on the bottom and being sent away from the group for a short period are good methods of creating associations of insecurity.

There is something else. Every action that is done by the parent to the child to create an association of insecurity with an action, also creates an association of insecurity toward the parent. This must be counteracted by other associations with the parent. For this reason the discipline must be mild enough to still leave an association of security with the parent. The parent must give the child security for no reason other than love so that the parent will be associated with security. Then the child will be concerned with the parent's attitude toward him. The child will feel his security is threatened if the parent is upset with him. And, he will know his security is protected if his parent is pleased with him.

If the child associates the parent with insecurity, he will associate insecurity with everything in the parent's environment, particularly those things the parent associates with security. The child will learn associations of insecurity from the parent, but he will not learn associations of security. His only associations of security will come from the removal of those things he associates with insecurity. This is not learning how to maximize security. It is learning how to minimize insecurity. After the child escapes his parents, he will have no knowledge of how to maximize his security. Indeed, he may have associations of insecurity with those associations and actions he needs the most. The opportunity for the parent to teach will have been ruined and the child may forever suffer because of it.

By associating security with the parent, the child also associates security with things in the parent's environment. If the parent dresses nicely, reads, and gives security to others; then the child will. He will associate a great amount of security with these things and he will grow up "right". This association of security with his parents will result in a good foundation for the child. He will have strong associations and strong restraints that will give him security.

When you are a child, you must be aware of the things you are being taught. They are for your own good; sometimes for your own safety. You must also be aware that the people who are teaching you are not greatly different from yourself. Children tend to think of parents as being perfect people who can handle everything. They are not, and it would do the child well to avoid causing his parents insecurity. Children who cause insecurity do not get the love and attention that good children get.

When the child gets older, children his own age, his peer group, become a significant source of security. This group will have associations and restraints that it will try to teach the child.

There are many social group opportunities for children of any given age. These groups are split by the things children that age associate with security. It may be academic achievement or athletic ability or clothing style or something else. If the child associates his parents with security, he will pick a group that associates security with the things his parents do. If he associates his parents with insecurity, he will tend to join a group that associates insecurity with the things his parents associate with security. Such a group may associate security with nothing except attacking the things it associates with insecurity, because it has no source of security except the removal of sources of insecurity.

Of course, there is the tendency to join the group containing people the child associates with security. If a pretty girl or good looking guy is in the group, others will tend to join it.

It is difficult for you to tell which group your child will try to join. The child who has security from his parents will be less dependent on the peer group as a source of security and, therefore, will not as easily accept their associations. You can only hope that your child's home life is such a strong source of security and he has such strong associations with your ideas that he will not accept the wrong group or the wrong associations of that group.

Society (the peer group) is one of the most dangerous sources of security when a person is too dependent on it. In a social group, each person is only one of many and is neither depended upon nor dependent upon any one other person. As a result, the individual who expresses a contrary opinion or acts differently, tends to be ignored. Members who find too great a security in society do not express opinions or act contrary to the group.

The peer group is not a bad source of security. It offers a source of security outside the home and is support and comfort when things go wrong. It gives advice and knowledge from the experiences of all. But, never follow the norms of society without question or without thinking. Association chains link society's rules. The first link may be okay, but the second may be a sin. Do not follow fads, ideas, or associations that you have not thought about.

Every source of security has to be watched for the associations it tries to create. Your associations must be first and foremost with God's laws. Associations contrary to those laws are not acceptable, because they will prevent you from maximizing your security. Because society is not perfect, sooner or later the rules of God will disagree with those of society. If the parents of the child have taught him the correct associations and have made themselves a good source of security, the child will find it much easier to follow God's laws and to use society properly as a source of security. Even though the Christian does not completely fit in, he will still have friends and will influence the social group closest to him.

Be sensitive to the effect you have on associations of others. Use initiative and good ideas to establish leadership (or at least influence).

Your Christian acts will give security to others and increase your influence. Remember, too, that society's rules are made by associations. Do not let someone get away with a statement that you do not agree with. You do not have to get into an argument, just let people know that you do not agree. The associations they have with you will then be used against any associations the other person was trying to create.

When you are a teenager, you must work hard to build the associations and restraints that are going to allow you to be successful in the grown-up world. If you are from a good home and a good peer group, this will be easier. But, remember, the world doesn't know who you are and it doesn't care what excuses you have. You make it in the real world based on your value to the security of the individuals in that world. There is no magic. There is no fairy godmother. It is only a question of how much you are associated with security and, ultimately, how much security you produce for others.

Excuses are not accepted. They do not mean anything. They have no value. They only lead you astray by making you believe that you do not have to improve. Excuses hide, from you, the solutions to your problems. The only thing in the universe that you can truly control is yourself. Take advantage of that! Maximizing security does not mean being rich or being loved. It only means that you will have food and shelter and you will make the best quality of life for yourself over time, given your starting environment. Remember, it is YOUR security.

The problems of growing up are caused by both parents and teenagers. Parents should be fair; they should try to see the other side of the question and think before they act. Teenagers are not children. Things should be suggested and reasons given. Parents should be careful to check and think whether they are speaking for their child's welfare or from their own past. The teenager must realize that he is responsible for himself. He must think before he acts and must not evade the real cause of a problem by blaming it on someone else. Poor upbringing is not a valid excuse for anything. Seek truth and be open-minded to parental ideas, but do not grab at every bit of wisdom. Even grownups are not perfect.

When you are a teenager, you must recognize your dependence on your parents. They are providing you with food and clothing while you are getting an education, learning those things that will allow you to gain security in the grown-up world. You are a burden on their time and finances, and they can stop providing their support. It is important that your parents associate you with security. Remember, "Honor thy parents". Never give your parents an ultimatum—they may take you up on it.

People, particularly the young, need knowledge, time, and security to develop the restraints and associations needed to maximize security. Of course, this is not always available. People can be poor and hungry. A bad environment makes the development of the proper tools nearly impossible. Fortunately, in the United States there is an education system that gives the government control of the child's environment for almost half his waking hours.

Here is the chance to give the child the knowledge of how to get along with others, to educate him into the culture so that he can be of benefit to his fellow man and be benefited by others. Here the child could have the relaxed, protected environment to gain the security and time that he could not have in his own environment. It is here that the resources of the whole society could be used to develop children so that they would not be held back by their home environment. In this way every child in the society would be able to develop to his fullest potential. All members of society would benefit tremendously.

It is sad to relate that this opportunity is wasted. Indeed, the school environment is often worse than the home environment. In the school the child is exposed to others of his age and older and a peer group which can be vicious toward the existing culture. Instead of a relaxed atmosphere with time to create necessary associations, the child is put under the pressure of getting good grades. The subjects that are taught are based too much on tradition; these are the subjects you take because this is what is taught in school. Furthermore, the child is given homework so that at home his time is spent doing routine schoolwork instead of acquiring security and developing restraints and associations.

Educated people are a benefit to the whole society. The educated tend to be more productive. They make more money. They pay more taxes. They are less likely to be criminals. The higher the percentage of the society that is educated, the better off everyone in the society will be.

Regardless of who the child's parents are, how much they make, and how much education they have, there is no absolute certainty that the child will become educated. Some do not have the mental ability, some do not have the motivation, and some do not have the opportunity because of their environment.

It is a great waste to the society to deny itself the opportunity to educate as many of its members as possible. A major objective of the education system must be to give everyone an equal opportunity to get an education.

The child needs an association of security with knowledge. Children whose home environment can not overcome the school environment, have trouble learning. Knowledge has hurt them, they know their grades make them lower class citizens among their school mates, and they associate knowledge with insecurity. This further hurts their ability to learn.

The student needs a good environment. He needs time to study and a low priority environment (peace and quiet so that he can concentrate). It is the job of the educational institution to provide this environment. Colleges have libraries which could be made more comfortable and relaxing. High schools have study hall courses, but they are usually noisy. To make matters worse, study halls do not last long enough.

The student needs to be taught how to learn. He needs to be taught how to study so that he will get maximum productivity from his study time.

There is too much homework and most of it seems to be some sort of scheme by the teachers. It is as if they are rewarded by the amount of work they give their students. Homework should be able to be done in the study hall at school. Study time should also be provided at school. No time for extra work or study should be required of the student at home. No homework! If necessary, make the school day longer.

Nothing destroys and distorts equal opportunity more than homework. It is one of the greatest social injustices because it bases opportunity on the student's home environment, instead of on his own ability.

The student's environment can be improved by giving him social opportunities. For some students, social life is their primary source of security. The school must teach them how to be sociable, particularly toward students of the opposite sex. Give the students dances and sporting events to attend. More importantly give them time at school to visit other students. There needs to be a social hour as well as a study hall.

The school system must teach students that which is relevant to their security. This requires the student to gain two kinds of knowledge.

First, a general knowledge of everything will give the student a better understanding of his world so that he can make better decisions and gain more security. The general knowledge should include all the different sciences (archaeology, nuclear physics) and arts (music, painting) as well as other subjects that are in today's university. General knowledge should include practical things such as how to change a tire and how to get along with other people. The student must be taught about sex. He must be taught about health—how to eat properly and how to recognize and handle diseases. He must be taught how a checking account works and what affects his credit rating. The student must be taught how to cook and how to find a place to live. He must learn to be diplomatic and polite. He must learn the laws. He must learn what government services are available so he can use them to maximize his security. (The government can help pay for college, for instance.) All those things that all parents had to learn from experience, much to their loss and regret, should be taught to the student.

Second, a specialized knowledge will allow the student to earn a living. The specialized knowledge should be in more than one area so that if one job field is full, the person can find a job in some other field. Too much work is required to be trained as a doctor and a lawyer, but the student could be trained in an unskilled job, a skilled job, and a professional job. Of course, these may have three different income levels, but some work is better than no job at all.

Educators must decide what is to be taught in each course. They should research the information available, then they should talk to educators designing the higher level courses and talk to the employers who will use their students. This will require a lot of time and effort. The knowledge to be taught needs to be reviewed periodically.

Learning is a matter of forming an association with that which is to be learned. The strength of the association depends on how much time is spent developing it and how much a factor it is in the environment. Of course, this means that the more the student has to study, the less time he will have for each fact and the less he will remember. This is why students wait until near test time to begin studying. There is so much to learn that the associations formed will be weak which means they can not be remembered for very long. The student ends up learning a lot of information that he retains for only a short period of time. He does retain that part of the knowledge that is repeated most often in the course.

What is the knowledge to be learned? An overview of the subject given first would help the student learn what facts and ideas were relevant to the overall knowledge to be learned in this subject. It would allow the student to associate the knowledge and ideas being taught in detail with an overall concept. This would make learning easier and time would not be wasted on unnecessary information. Is this what is wrong with the way chemistry is taught today?

Unnecessary information will not be learned. Much of the detail information that students are taught is never remembered. Employees who use that detail in their job always look it up in a reference manual. There is no purpose in trying to learn that detail. Instead, the student should be taught where and how to look it up. He must also be taught how and when to use the information. This means that the student should be taught the theory and shown some usages of the theory. He should be required to show an ability to use the theory. This can be done by working mathematical problems, answering hypothetical social science problems with essays, etc. This is the information that should be learned.

At present colleges feel that all the world's knowledge can be divided into course of 12 or 17 weeks (the quarter or semester system). This says that the English student needs to know as much beginning chemistry as the chemistry student. The chemistry student has strong associations toward chemistry that the English student does not have. Furthermore, a whole semester of chemistry is probably not needed by the English student. The English student gets bored, has poor associations causing him to learn less, and he gets poorer grades in beginning chemistry (causing a voter to associate insecurity with a whole area of knowledge). Because he does not have strong associations with chemistry and its ideas, it will take the English student longer to grasp the concepts being taught in chemistry. Courses should be divided into areas of relevant information. The chemistry and English students would still take the first chemistry course. However, it would require only the general knowledge needed by the English student. Such a course may only last a few weeks, if that is all that is needed.

Instead of trying to get the student to remember a lot of information over a short period of time, the course should be set up to teach the student a definite amount of knowledge. At the beginning of the course, the student should be informed with written questions and answers, exactly what he is to learn in the course. The tests will be on this written information, perhaps with some questions required and others selected at random. Instead of one test on one day, there should be several tests on the same information over a given time period. This requires the student to study the knowledge over a longer period of time, thus acquiring a stronger association. After the student has graduated, his certification for a course should last only for a given period of time. He should be required to take the test again (with updated knowledge) every four years or so.

When what is taught is relevant to maximizing security, the student should be required to learn it before he is considered to have passed the course. In today's school, the student has to acquire a percentage of the knowledge (sometimes as low as 60%) or he must learn as much as most of the other students (this is called grading on the curve). Knowing 65% of the answers on a test that is not relevant to your security is fine, but it is not good enough if you know only 65% of what you need to acquire and maximize security in the real world. All students should get A's.

Courses must be taught with a technique that develops associations with the knowledge to be learned. The teacher must make the knowledge to be learned a major part of the classroom environment. For instance, to teach that George Washington was the first president, a movie could be shown of his life or a story told of the early years of the United States. The student would not be required to learn the dates of Washington's birth, marriage, or death. But, he would have learned easily that Washington was the first president.

It is easier to develop associations with knowledge if it is intellectually stimulating (fun, makes the student feel good, gives him security). Boredom creates an association of insecurity toward knowledge. Boring knowledge makes less secure students give up on knowledge as a source of security. If history is a series of dates, it is boring. If it is an exciting story, it is security. If chemistry is memorizing formulas, it is boring. If it is knowledge of the complex interplay of materials in our environment, it is useful, practical information that can be used by the student to increase his own security.

Educational institutions and methods should be many things. The institution must provide a suitable environment for the student. He should be taught how to study and how to be sociable. He must be provided with an environment in which to study. He must be provided with an environment with which to gain security from society. Methods must teach specialized and general knowledge that allow the student to maximize his security. The student must be required to learn the knowledge expected of him before he is given credit for a course. The course must require only the information the student needs. The present failure to meet these requirements costs society opportunity to gain security for us all.

When you are a student, it is your responsibility to use the educational opportunity to develop the knowledge and skills that you can use to maximize your security over time. There are a lot of intellectually stimulating subjects. They are fun, but you still have to eat and support a family. Include in your course load something that will get you a job.

Incidentally, for those of you who don't want to go to school, there is a hard reality to education. The reality is that if you don't get a good education, you won't get a good job and without a good job, you will have trouble getting and keeping a spouse. I don't care what it's like—stay in school.

Of course, there is more to life than hanging out with friends and going to school.

Chapter Twelve

LOVE AND MARRIAGE

Marriage used to be based on economics, and still is in most cultures. The woman would clean the house, do the laundry, and fix meals. The man would earn the money to buy the food and pay the rent. Each needed the other as an economic necessity. Each spouse would be willing to endure a lot of insecurity from the other before the marriage would end, because each needed the standard-of-living security that the other provided. When the marriage environment was a source of insecurity, the rich would have affairs and the poor would drink or go crazy.

In the modern United States, both the man and woman work to earn money. The house cleaning and child raising are shared and the cooking is done by restaurants. This means that the man and woman do not need each other economically as much as they once did and that means that marriages end more easily. For the modern American, keeping the marriage together depends a great deal on maintaining an environment of security with affection, sex, and relaxation.

Is this bad? If marriage in previous generations was based on economics and we must base it on quality of life; if we learn, aren't we going to have a better quality of life?

Nothing is better than romance. Maybe for the first time in our lives we learn that there are great rewards for being nice to others. Our whole outlook on life changes from self-centered dealings with our peers and parents to being a partner and friend to someone we care about in a much more caring way than we have felt before. It's great, even if it is emotionally disturbing. It takes us out of our self-centered universe and gives us sensitivity, an attitude of caring for others, and a joy for life.

Romance is not easy to come by. It may start with physical attractiveness; and, although that is not necessary, it doesn't hurt. Even if you can not change your face or height, you can control your weight and you can keep clean and dress nicely. Actually, romance requires a certain attitude on your part to begin with. There has to be a certain level of kindness toward other people and a certain degree of sensitivity toward the feelings of others and a certain degree of tolerance.

In our society there are pressures against romance. There are economic pressures. For instance, it is considered acceptable for parents to cut off funds to students who marry, although the parents would have continued to support the students if they had not married. Parents who want to help can not get student loans for married children, and the parent's health insurance no longer covers the student once they are married.

There are social pressures. People will tell you that you should date many people and have many "experiences" before deciding on marriage. There may be some truth to that. It is as if we were trying to decide how good-looking or rich a partner we could get before settling for someone. I suppose the thought is that if we got better-looking and richer after marriage we would give up the first partner and find something better.

Love is not such a great matter of age and comparison. Security in a love relationship is not only a matter of beauty and party personality. Obviously, there are people over forty who are in love with one another and who do not get divorced whenever they see someone who is twenty years younger. Love between two people is an exchange of security; they stay together because one is dependent upon the other for security. This security is caused by sharing, understanding, and sympathy. It is not true that older people fall in love easier. Younger people are better looking and feel more insecure. For them, the need is greater and so is the attraction. Furthermore, older people tend to have stronger associations. (Strength is a matter of time and they have had their associations longer.) Younger people can adjust more easily to a partner; love can have a greater affect on their associations.

Society benefits from the positive accomplishments of individuals. The pressure against marriage causes some people to wait. While they wait, they are not acquiring the security they could have had, and they are not developing the associations they need to do something extraordinary. Time is lost. Society loses what it could have gained, if the person had developed faster.

Keeping a romance requires more than a spark of attractiveness and some quiet evenings. We all like to think that romance is magic, and, if the feeling is with us now, nothing else matters now or in the future. Although some of us believe in the magic, at least some of the time, very few of us believe in it all of the time. No matter how attractive and fun someone is, there should be moments of thought and reflection.

Is this relationship going to allow you to maximize your security in the present and future environment? Does the partner provide a potential standard of living? Does the partner have a Christian set of values? Is the partner a nice person? Do each of you think ahead? How will you and your partner handle stress? Will each of you support the other?

I think that usually at least one of the potential partners considers these things early in the relationship and breaks it off before there is serious emotional involvement. If a relationship will not provide security, it picks up a bad association and ends. It is the potential long-range security from the relationship that each partner should consider. This is what your parents and friends look at when they comment on your date.

Of course, it is helpful to remember that no one is perfect. (It is sad that for the most important decision we will make in our lives, we have so little training from our education system.)

In these days when men and women can marry whomever they want, love and romance are a necessary part of human nature both to attract the other sex and to decide whom to marry.

The truth about love and romance is that each spouse must provide security to the other during the entire course of the marriage, or the marriage will fail; not just what we perceive to be security, but real security. I want to believe in true love lasting forever, no matter what. I want to believe that if you marry the right person, that one person for you, that you will live happily ever after. It is not so, and that is disappointing. But, I am trying to write what I perceive, not what I want life to be.

You can be good looking and charming and win someone's love, but you can not keep it unless you can provide security to your spouse: money, a home, food, clothing, and an environment with minimum insecurity. If there is no real security, the insecurity of the environment will create associations of insecurity with everything in the environment, including you. Courtship is an escape from reality to anticipation of sex and affection. The other truth, the reality of marriage, is that marriage is the result of associations with romance being linked with the associations of your day-to-day environment.

Love is romance and mystery and anticipation; marriage is the grim reality of living together; and marriage can be more fun. No longer do you each have to go to separate homes after a date; you wake up beside each other. You don't have to worry about getting too physically involved; you can make love anytime you want to—morning, afternoon, or night. You no longer have to call on the phone if you want to just talk. People get married because they associate marriage with affection, sex, security, and relaxation (a low stress environment). Marriage can give you everything you anticipated during courtship.

You must continue to date after marriage. You must go out together and do fun things together. You must take vacations together. You must have fun together. Each must be a part of the security in the other's life. Just by sharing a secure environment, you strengthen your associations of security with each other.

One of the advantages of marriage is its affect on the influence of society. Marriage provides an alternative source of security. It can allow a person to be more of an individual; a person less curbed in his search for security. The association of insecurity with being different in the eyes of society will not be as strong. We are all brought up in a culture that expects certain things of us. Very often, that expectation tries to keep us "in our place". It prevents us from doing what we want to do. It prevents us from bettering ourselves and our children. The married person is able to seek to maximize his security with less difficulty. The associations of security with society's rules are weaker for him than for others who have to rely on society for security.

A secure environment is essential to a marriage. Stress from outside the marriage and from inside (money problems, etc.) can break the marriage. Stress lowers the security level and thereby overcomes restraints. This can result in partners causing each other insecurity.

Some people think marriage will solve all their problems, but they find that loneliness and sexual desire are replaced by the problems of money and getting along with a roommate. It may sometimes seem that sex with another person will solve your problems or leaving the marriage will solve your problems. Neither is true. The only way to solve a problem is to attack it. Sex with another person will only weaken the marriage. Use the strength of the marriage to solve problems. Make a time of peace and quiet to study your association chains to find the solution and then develop the associations to solve the problem.

Sex has the potential to put a strong association of security into the marriage environment. If you commit adultery, you will weaken the strength of that association. Associations with sex are dangerous because if following your associations causes your partner insecurity, they will begin to associate insecurity with you and their relationship with you. Needless to say, when the association of security with sex goes out of the marriage, the marriage is in big trouble.

One imagined problem is the idea that the other partner's search for individual development will give him sources of security that will ruin the marriage. Will he like fishing so much that he will stay at the lake and never come home? Will she like opera so much that she will run off with the first tenor? The individual's search to maximize his own security will not hurt the marriage. Each partner's greatest source of security is the other partner. He does not want to sleep with fish. She does not want to live with someone who does not understand her as well as her husband does. If the marriage is drifting apart, he may spend more time fishing and she more time at the opera, but fishing and opera are not the problems. They are just the symptoms of the disease. The problem is in the strength of the associations between the partners. The solution is to find what is weakening those associations.

Let the other partner develop as he will. You must develop as you want to. Always remember to develop to maximize your security. By "develop" I do not mean to go out and sin to your heart's content. I do mean to have hobbies, to take night school courses, go to ball games, whatever. Each partner should be given time to do these things. It is important that each partner be given this time, for this is where the individual feels that he is free and independent. Indeed, he is more independent than the single person. He has a dependable sex life and the services his marriage partner provides. Would you rather go to a ball game or to a sewing class feeling sexually frustrated and lonely or would you rather go feeling content?

There are times when the individual's development activities are done alone, but they can also be done with the partner. Each should take an interest in what the other is doing and participate if asked. A wife may need her husband to escort her to the opera. Sometimes a man likes to go fishing with friends, sometimes alone, and sometimes with his wife.

The marriage must not limit security. Each partner must respect the other's need to be an individual. (Remember that we are each seeking what we perceive to be our own security.) Otherwise, the marriage limits security and conflict exists where it should not.

Problems in a marriage make it difficult to communicate, but communication is the best way to solve a problem. Communication must not be seen as the beginning of a confrontation. It must be seen as the solution to a source of insecurity. Good communicating can beat problems before they start. Be honest and understanding of the feelings (associations) of your partner. When associations of insecurity occur (fights, getting mad at each other), try to correct those insecurities as soon as possible (apologize, bring her flowers, fix him a nice dinner).

As a person develops, he changes. His associations change and what he associates with security changes. You need to know those new associations so that you can give security. You also need to know how you must change so that your partner still associates you with security (do you need to change the way you dress, do you need to improve your knowledge on some new subject?). You need to know what security your partner needs (peace and quiet, friendship and good times at a party, etc.). You need to know what things are causing your partner insecurity. These same things you must also know about yourself.

Then you and your partner must communicate these things to each other. You must decide how much security (or insecurity) is attached to each thing and work out the best course of action to maximize each person's security. All this requires honest communication between partners, and that is difficult.

Communication is done by talking. The talking is to develop new associations in your partner and in yourself. Creating new associations and destroying old ones requires time. One conversation does not give a person time to sort through his associations and change his mind. One conversation probably does not allow a person to go through his associations to comprehend or reply. One conversation, one apology is not enough! Do not expect your partner to change based on one discussion. Do not expect your partner to adequately reply in one discussion. You must have continuing discussions so that each person has an opportunity to sift through their associations regarding the conversation topic. (Each needs time to think about it.)

Communication is frightening. Just bringing up subjects that are critical to your relationship means putting the relationship at risk because if the subject means a great deal to you, your partner's rejection will mean a great deal of insecurity to you and will cause a strong association of insecurity toward your partner and toward the relationship. But, no one enters a relationship with the intention of ending it. Chances are that the subject that means so much to you, does not mean that much to your partner. If it did, you would have seen that conflict early in the relationship. (You did talk first, didn't you?)

Making assumptions about your partner is not communicating! That is the old way of being married when there was an economic relationship and each behaved as their parents had behaved. If they were lucky, they would have a happy marriage, but it was just luck against long odds. An assumption is judging the other person and it's a sin. An assumption is a lost opportunity. Communication by conversation will show each partner the means to acquire security and to give it.

You must never judge your partner. If the husband likes ballet and the wife thinks it is unmanly, she must change her associations. She must never make fun of him or the ballet. When you judge the other person and attack their sources of security, you create two associations of insecurity within that person. One is against you. The other is against the source of security. (The ballet will not give the husband as much security if the wife keeps telling him it is unmanly.) It is unfair of you and damaging to your marriage to create associations of insecurity in your partner toward his other sources of security. If you criticize him for going to the ball game or criticize her for playing bridge with the girls, you are decreasing the amount of security that your partner will get from that activity. Your partner will then not get his security because of his marriage and he will begin to associate the marriage with insecurity. This is a hazard to the marriage. Judging your partner does you no good and only decreases his security.

Chances are that your spouse's associations that seem so important are irrelevant to you. They do not affect you and will not affect you. They may be contrary to your associations so you will feel insecurity toward them, but they do not concern you, so leave them alone. We are all individuals and we associate security with the way we do things, but being individuals means we do some things that are different. So, your partner is going to do things differently from the way you do and is going to have different associations. That just makes things interesting. Do not get lead around by your associations to the extent that you try to impose them on your partner when your partner's associations are not relevant to your security.

As in all things, you should work to maximize your own security, but especially if you are married. Remember, your partner associates you with security. If you are unhappy and obviously feeling insecure, your partner will also feel insecure. This is not good because it makes for an insecure environment which is associated with the relationship. Your partner knows that the only reason he is feeling insecure is because you are. We can't be happy all the time, but if you have a source of insecurity in your life, solve it. Don't just tolerate it and hope it will go away. Make a plan of action to get out of debt or find a new job or move to a better neighborhood.

Whatever is needed, make a plan and work toward it. That will make you feel better and will improve your partner's security.

Keep yourself sexually attractive. It is important to your partner. Avoid fatigue. When you are tired, you are working on a higher priority level and your actions are not as well controlled by your associations. This may well result in actions that cause insecurity to your partner.

If you get divorced, behave yourself. Your marriage vows may have ended, but God and His laws still exist. You do yourself much harm by being vindictive to someone you once loved. The associations that creates in you and in others toward you are very harmful.

The way to protect your marriage is to maintain the environment of affection, sex, security, and relaxation that lead you both to get married in the first place.

Chapter Thirteen

JOB AND MONEY

To have a standard of living, we need money which means we need a job. The trick is to get the best job—and keep it. Jesus says the worker is worthy of his hire, so you have to make yourself worthy.

Your worth to your company is how productive you are. If you are a salesman, how much do you sell? Is the product easy to sell or difficult to sell? If you are a manager, how difficult are the decisions you make and how much affect do they have on the company's profit? If you are a manufacturer, how skilled are you, how much product do you make, and how difficult are you to replace?

Your worth is affected by the laws of supply and demand. If you dig ditches, but so does everyone else who is looking for a job, then you have limited worth because you can easily be replaced. This is why people with more education and more experience usually have more value.

The statement "worthy of hire" also refers to companies. Whether the company does well is determined by the value of its product to the community.

Your worth is tied to the value of your company as well as to the worth of your own services to that company. The most valued employee of a company that is out of business, is out of a job.

In deciding upon a career there are three things to consider. First, how do you make yourself valuable to your company. Second, which companies are most valuable to the community so they will remain in business. Third, what is going to maximize your security—money is not everything! A high stress job that pays lots of money may not maximize your security. On the other hand, some higher paying jobs give better benefits; fewer hours, better retirement, and health care.

Work toward your future. Too many people think education means sitting in class until they are old enough to get a job. "Value to the company" depends on your knowledge and skills. Knowledge comes from education and experience. Your skills come from experience and your own developed abilities. The most important skill is an ability to get along with people and communicate with them. Needless to say, following the laws of Jesus will handle that problem.

Attitude and work habits are critical to your value. It is a shame these things never seem to be taught in school. If your parents know these things and teach them to you, if these things are a part of your culture, you will probably do well earning a living. Otherwise, with no one to teach you correct business behavior, you will probably do as well as those who taught you the rest of your culture. A society must give equal opportunity to its members and equal opportunity means equal access to critical knowledge. Failure to do this limits the society's potential for productivity.

When the student leaves school he is told that things are different in the real world. They are and the difference is humiliation. No matter how prepared you are, you will make mistakes or you will not know something that the experienced workers know. How you react to this is important to you. If you can swallow your pride and learn, you will be well on your way to developing yourself into a valuable employee. If you react by associating insecurity with your job and fellow employees, you will not learn, you will be a burden on the company, and you will cost yourself opportunities for security.

It is on the job, as much as any place, where all those rules we discussed earlier become so apparent as laws of the real environment. Be humble so you can learn and improve yourself. Be meek so you do not offend your fellow employees. Do not judge others—you have to work with them and be polite and inoffensive toward them. No where can "love your enemy" be more devastating than in the workplace where a smile and friendly, "hello" can be confusing to people who thought they did not like you. Be a peacemaker, one who can settle disputes and keep people working together. Thirst to see right prevail, because, despite all the talk and politics, the ultimate goal of the work group is to provide something of value to the society. If you have the influence, let your work group know the things they are doing that are of value to the society and the things they are doing that are not of value.

Management must make its workers feel secure. Employees must have the opportunity to gain security by working. In addition to wages and benefits, this is generally done by salary increases each year and retirement plans. Training and classes for new technology in the work place help. Set specific rules of performance so that the worker will know that if he is within those rules he will not have to worry. Giving the employee security means that he will be better able to develop associations and actions. He will have a better life at home and he will do better work. The employee, the community, and the company will all benefit.

The individual, in maximizing his own security, must make some confusing decisions concerning his job. On the one hand, there is the need for the standard of living that the job provides. On the other hand, there is the group responsibility concept of Christianity that prevents being part of a group not acting in a Christian manner.

I must qualify this. Everyone thinks that someone above him in management is incompetent. We all think that at least some of our bosses are stupid, lazy, or insensitive. However, just because we have an association of insecurity with management, we should not conclude that they are sinners and that group responsibility dictates that we must leave the organization. You must not judge others. Look at their actions.

Is your organization increasing or decreasing the security of society? I am sure that every company does things that are wrong, just as every person does things that are wrong. One sin does not evaluate the whole company. The group responsibility decision to stay or go depends on two things. First, if the company is increasing the security of society (even if not maximizing it), then it is probably a good company and you should not leave because of group responsibility. The second factor is the company's response to you. If you are associated with security and they listen to you, then you should stay unless the small advances you are making can not hope to soon overcome the insecurity to society being done by the company.

Leaving a company for group responsibility reasons may seem to be contrary to maximizing your own security, but money is only one aspect of security. If you work for a bad company, you must leave or get stuck with the insecurity of group responsibility. As for the money, God will provide it. If you are a Christian, you are valuable because you give security. You will find another job even if you have to move to another place. Group responsibility or not, you have an absolute responsibility to yourself. Never, ever, commit a sin because the company wants you to do so.

We have a very strong association of security with money. If you are not thoughtful, if you are in a hurry, money is dangerous. Its strong association gives it influence and it creeps into our decision making and leads us away from the laws of God.

The question regarding money is: how much of your time should be spent in acquiring the standard of living security? Similarly, how much time should be spent with family, how much with friends, how much in acquiring accomplishments?

Money can be a powerful tool, if you manage it. It can allow you to change careers and find a more security-giving job, but only if you have saved it and do not have such a large monthly budget that you can not afford a reduction in salary. If you have invested wisely, it can ultimately give you the freedom to work as you wish and do as you wish (as long as you do not sin).

God's promise to mankind is to provide food and shelter in exchange for following Jesus. The Christian will always be worthy of his hire because of his ability to handle conflict and to not decrease the security of others.

Chapter Fourteen

SUFFERING AND DEATH

If there is a loving God, why is there suffering and death? This, more than anything else, must lead people to question the existence of God and His love for mankind. The reason for death and suffering is irrelevant. Jesus does not tell us why they exist, only how to deal with them.

Jesus says you will suffer persecution for His sake, and we have discussed that, but what if you are in pain from some physical condition? Maximize your security by getting what comfort you can. Realize, nevertheless, that suffering does not relieve you of the obligation to follow God's laws—be nice to others. More than at any time, you must do this. If you do not, you may lose the services of those who are giving you comfort.

Even if the reasons are irrelevant, why, in the grand design of the universe, is there suffering and death? I would like to speculate as to its purpose.

We have heard stories of the rich and powerful who have suffered in pain and agony from terrible diseases. We have heard stories of the great and good who have had tragedy and suffering in their lives. You may or may not experience suffering no matter who you are, no matter how good or bad. Perhaps suffering and death help to give us a hard reminder that we must work with reality. No amount of wishing will relieve us that responsibility, whether we attack it or it attacks us. The laws of Jesus are there to help us deal with the real environment, but there is no magic that will allow us to avoid it.

Suffering and death should also tell you there is no one better than you, the individual. If others suffer as you may, doesn't that mean that you can aspire to the things they aspire to? Doesn't that mean that you have within you the capability of accomplishing the things they accomplished? Suffering and death teach us that there are no second-class human beings. We are all in this together—equally.

Death gives each of us a time limit; a certainty that this will all end. We can not delay forever the things we wish to do in life. If we are to accomplish something, we need to get started. If you believe in Jesus, you know your sins can be forgiven, if you ask; but you may die at any time, so perhaps you should not sin and count on forgiveness before you die.

Suffering and death cause us insecurity because they hurt and destroy our sources of security. This association of insecurity with suffering and death is a key ingredient in the insecurity the individual will receive by decreasing the security of others. Suffering and death are a deterrent to people causing insecurity to others.

If people were immortal, power would continue to lie with those persons who favored the current rules of society. Those who wanted change would not be able to generate any influence. With death, those people who were brought up in one culture will be replaced by those brought up in a newer culture. The rules of society may not change, but at least the tools are there to provide the opportunity.

There does not appear to be any divine reason why people die when they do. Sometimes death is just an unfortunate circumstance. Anyone can have a plane crash into their house or be killed by a mad sniper. Of course, there is still the natural law of survival of the fittest. People who can not obey rules, such as traffic laws, have a greater chance of being killed than those who can. With all God's love for man, it must seem strange that He cares so little about death.

The fact is that God really does care very little about death. For instance, there is the statement by Jesus that you should not fear death, but him who can kill the soul. God does not care about death because it is irrelevant. When a person dies, he is gone. He never returns. His relationship to the living and the laws of human behavior is at an end. The dead do not fight the war of life. They are retired. There is no sorrow by the dead for their death. They are not in pain. They are not lonely. They have suffered no loss of security. Security is no longer relevant to them.

The relevance of death is to the living, and, to this, Jesus says to leave the dead to bury their dead. Do not mourn those who are no longer with us. Christianity is present and future. There is no past in Christianity. It does not matter that you killed a little girl who ran in front of your car. It does not matter that your spouse of 25 years is dead.

What matters is that you do your best to follow the teachings of Jesus now and in the future. If you allow the past to affect your present by mourning a tragedy, you are sinning. You are decreasing your own security by thinking of insecure associations, and, while you are doing that, you are not increasing the security of those around you. If you think of the good times you had with the person who died, that will give you security. However, if you think of the dead instead of finding other sources of security, you will not be maximizing your security.

Jesus does not say why there is suffering and death. The "why" is irrelevant. We have to live with these things—they are part of life. Go on living, maximizing your security in spite of them.

Chapter Fifteen

CONCLUSION

What are we doing here? What are we supposed to be doing here? If we were created, then we are to do whatever it is we are created to do. And, we are to do it well.

We perceive that we make decisions. It does not matter that some Creator may have programmed all this, so He knows what decision we will make—we do not know.

We are living organisms which react chemically to internal and external stimuli. To have survived long enough to reproduce and continue the species, we must react to the environment in such a way that we, as individuals, live long enough to reproduce. There must be something in the way we are built that allows us to feel good when we receive a stimulus that is good for us and feel bad when we receive a bad stimulus. Stimuli that make us feel good give us a feeling of security. Things that make us feel bad give us a feeling of insecurity.

The problem is that we react to the environment as we perceive it in that one moment of time. We may use our associations from the past to determine how we will react, but we are living in the present as we perceive it. The danger to us is the environment we do not perceive in the present and the environment of the future which we can guess at, but can not perceive at all.

What are we to do? As we live from day-to-day, we develop certain associations and actions as we react to our environment, trying to adapt to gain security. This means our associations and actions tend to be forced on us by our environment. However, we can strengthen and weaken our associations and thereby control our actions. We can read and listen and learn and we can use what we learn to guide us in changing the strengths of our associations. This is our great gift as human beings. We can control ourselves because we are not limited by the associations and their strengths as imposed on us by our external environment. We can seek to maximize our security over time. What is needed is an absolute set of associations that will provide the maximum amount of security in every possible situation.

When we look at physics and chemistry, we get the impression that the universe has been designed, created in a deliberate fashion with set laws so that everything works together. If the universe is designed, there may be rules for human behavior.

These rules, if we can make our own decisions and if we seek what we perceive to be our security, must maximize our security over time. Furthermore, if we are to make our own decisions, the laws of human behavior can not be forced upon us. They are not written on the sky or on a mountain that does not touch the ground. The definition of the existence of these laws must have a certain degree of vagueness. So, if someone says they have the natural laws of human behavior, how do we know they are really the laws? We are looking for a description of reality, not just what we perceive, but what is relevant to us now and in the future.

Science discovers the real environment by defining natural laws, each of which is an "invariable association" between "events or properties" about which there is "universal agreement". Scientific theories explain the natural laws and use that explanation to define new laws. The explanation in a theory takes the form of an analogy with a theory whose laws are known and recognized. An accurate theory must describe the real environment (now and in the future) and have a wider scope than other, contrary, theories. It does not matter how the laws were "discovered". It only matters that they are accurate.

There are three security theories. These describe how man acts and how he should act. The first theory is that each individual human being seeks what he perceives to be his own individual security. This is based on an analogy with biological laws. The second theory is that each individual should seek to maximize his own security over time. This is an analogy with the first theory of security. The third theory of security is that Jesus Christ gave man the Natural Laws of Human Behavior and only by following those laws can the individual maximize his security over time. This is also an analogy with the first theory of security. A theory must be able to predict new laws. The new law of the third theory of security is that the individual can not maximize his security over time by decreasing someone else's security.

SOME RULES OF GOD

Strengthening the Individual

Build Associations with God
> Love God; Worship and serve only God; Do the will of God; Call no man your Father on earth; Do not swear; Do not deny Jesus; Do not speak against the Holy Ghost.

Resist Attempts to Alter Your Associations with God
> Have no other gods; Have no idols; Do not take the name of God in vain; Give alms to God in secret; Fast in private; Pray in private.

Rewards to the Individual
> Do not worry about food or drink; Take no thought of what to say; Ask and you will receive; Seek and you will find.

Rules to Seek Maximum Security
> Do not tempt God; Always be ready for God; Do not covet anything that is your neighbor's; Do not mourn the dead; Get

married if you are ready for it; Do not work on the sabbath; Be pure in heart; Be perfect.

Rules to Evaluate Others

Honor thy father and thy mother; Know false prophets by the results of their actions.

Rules to Develop Proper Associations Toward Others

Do not judge others; Be humble; Mourn; Love your enemy; Bless them that curse you.

Relating to Others

Violence

Turn the other cheek; Be wise as serpents, harmless as doves; When you are persecuted in one town, move on; Suffer persecution; Do not kill; Beware of men.

Group conflict

Teach; Go and teach all nations, baptizing them; If your brother sins, talk, go to church, ignore him; Allow children to learn of God; Do not be called master; Let your light shine.

Individual Conflict

Love your neighbor; Give when asked; If sued, settle quickly; Be meek; Be merciful; Forgive; Treat others as you would have them treat you; Do not steal; Do not bear false witness against your neighbor; Do not commit adultery; Adultery is looking with lust; Adultery is marrying a woman divorced, not for adultery; Adultery is divorce and remarry; Do not disrupt a marriage; Be reconciled with your brother; Be a peacemaker; Want that which is right to prevail.

The Creator of the Universe made the religion just as certainly as He made the science. They are not opposites. There is no such thing in the real environment as a choice between religion and science. They are part of the same universe, the same finely intertwined set of laws.